America's Living Past

America's Living Past

HISTORIC VILLAGES & RESTORATIONS

JOHN BOWEN

Portland House
New York

This 1990 edition was published by Portland House, a division of di-lithium Press, Ltd., distributed by Outlet Book Company Inc, a Random House Company, 225 Park Avenue South, New York, New York 10003.

8 7 6 5 4 3 2 1

ISBN 0-517-69475-1

Printed and bound in Hong Kong

America's Living Past was prepared and produced by M & M Books, 11 W. 19th Street, New York, New York 10011

An M&M book

Project Director & Editor   Gary Fishgall

Senior Editorial Assistant   Shirley Vierheller; Editorial Assistants David Blankenship, Ben D'Amprisi, Jr., Maxine Dormer, Grace Sullivan, Ben McLaughlin, Lisa Pike; Copy Editor   Bert N. Zelman of Publishers Workshop Inc.

Photo Research   David Blankenship

Designer   Binns & Lubin/Martin Lubin

Separations and Printing   Regent Publishing Services Ltd.

Typesetting   Village Type & Graphics

CONTENTS

(Previous Pages) **Making parts to replace worn-out equipment was a continuing job for 19th-century craftsmen like this one at Living History Farms in Des Moines, Iowa.**

(These Pages) **Broad-brimmed Brothers hats add a decorative touch to the spare but attractive environs of Hancock Shaker Village.**

Introduction   6

The Emerging Nation   8

The Developing Nation   40

A Nation Divided   68

The Western Frontier   96

The Maturing Nation   156

Additional Information   190

Credits and Acknowledgements   192

A Nation of Collectors

More than 150 years ago, French social philosopher Alexis de Tocqueville correctly discerned that the need for change was a guiding force in American life. What he could not foresee was a conservative streak, persistent in American history. As Henry Wadsworth Longfellow said, "our todays and yesterdays are the blocks with which we build." This reverence for what we have been, as well as what we are, has made us a nation of collectors, both as individuals and as a society.

Calls for historic preservation emerged in the 19th century, even as the nation was moving the frontier ever westward, and became quite vocal by the late 1800s. However, action did not always follow desire, and, during most of the 19th century, activity was confined to erecting monuments and memorials. While preservation of sites like the Saratoga battlefield was stressed during the centennial celebration in 1877, the site was not actually acquired until 1923.

The 20th century has been different. Numerous individual Americans and governments at all levels—local, state and national—as well as many private associations are inveterate, often indiscriminate, collectors. Historical attractions that survived by accident have been retrieved. Individual initiative created some collections so large that public display became the only rational course of action. So much has been collected, restored, and reconstructed that more than 300 historic landmarks, large and small, dot the landscape from east to west and north to south. They re-create the diverse American experience in its many varied stages, although they seldom can be viewed chronologically in any single area. Some are easily accessible near interstate routes; others are tucked away in coastal enclaves and isolated mountain areas.

These are not static facilities; in action and living color, they tell the fascinating story of how America became what it is. Want to witness a Revolutionary encampment or a Civil War battle? Ample opportunities exist, stretching from Boston to New Mexico. What about the lifestyles of the past? They are manifest from Jamestown and Colonial Williamsburg in Virginia through the Boot Hill Museum in Kansas to the goldfield towns of California. Daily life is depicted as it was, warts and all, in humble log cabins, plantation mansions, simple business offices, and crammed country stores, as well as farmlands where people eked out a living from the American soil. Large museums, like the Henry Ford Museum and Greenfield Village, reveal the passion for variety that has characterized all of American history. Folk art, until a few generations ago the avocation of the few, has become the wonder of the many—and today many fine collections, like the one at Shelburne, Vermont, flourish.

To a large extent, the urge to preserve and re-create the best of the past derives from a feeling that new generations ought to be able to understand and appreciate their heritage.

Arthur Hazelius, who in 1872 invented the open-air museum concept at Skansen in Stockholm, Sweden, was concerned that the gentle, individualistic way of life he had known as a child was disappearing. The open-air museum was an idea whose time had come, and soon it spread to Norway, Denmark, and the Netherlands. The concept took hold gradually in the United States, starting in the 1920s. According to Gerald George, director of the American Association for State and Local History, the first open-air historical museum in the United States was at Essex Institute in Salem, Massachusetts. Schoenbrun, a Moravian log village in Ohio which opened in 1923, also was among the earliest. The restoration of Colonial Williamsburg under the patronage of John D. Rockefeller, Jr., began in 1926. Henry Ford began putting together the complex that became the Henry Ford Museum and Greenfield Village in 1929. In recent decades, the momentum to save our heritage has accelerated, thanks in part to a general increase in leisure time and the resultant rise in tourism.

There are two kinds of open-air museums: the chronological/comparative type, such as the Genesee County Museum near Rochester, New York, covers more than one historical period, whereas the "slice-of-the-past" museum, such as Plimoth Plantation, depicts a specific place in a specific time. Likewise, two development patterns are used: one in which restoration and reconstruction take place on the historic site itself, as at Colonial Williamsburg; the other, where representations in the form of old buildings are moved from their original sites and assembled somewhere else to create a specific theme museum, such as the Farmers' Museum in Cooperstown, New York, or to cover a broader spectrum, as at the Shelburne Museum in Vermont.

In like manner, the preservation of battlefields and other sites of historical moment was much discussed and seldom acted upon until the present century. Now, the two greatest wars which were fought on U.S. territory—the Revolutionary War and the Civil War—are vividly recalled at many of the major combat sites. In addition, historical presentations cover everything from the home of an admired politician to the place where the Declaration of Independence and the U.S. Constitution were written.

At most sites, living history demonstrations have become an integrated part of the program. Interpreters and role players in period dress use authentic tools and equipment in the old-fashioned way to demonstrate how people lived, played, worked, and fought.

The sites, reenactments, encampments, and other activities explored in this book are a cross section of the best that is available to every American citizen. A place is occasionally discussed in several different chapters, if it represents more than one of the broad historical periods covered herein. In most instances, however, the entire review of a site may be found in the chapter devoted to the primary area of focus. Together, the places examined in this volume represent a significant segment of our cultural history. If the signposts of the future lie in the past, the United States is marking its route well.

(*Opposite*) Stereoscopes, sometimes viewed by lamp light, gave turn-of-the-century families a window on the world. This example comes from Living Histroy Farms in Des Moines, Iowa.

The Emerging Nation

PLIMOTH PLANTATION

The first voyage of Christopher Columbus to the New World in 1492 stirred the competitive juices of Western Europe's principal nations. In addition to Columbus's three subsequent voyages, other Spanish explorers sought to propagate the Roman Catholic faith while searching for gold (Columbus, in fact, was an Italian who sailed for Spain). French explorers entered Canada and descended the mighty rivers into what is now the American Midwest. French Huguenots, seeking to escape religious persecution, created settlements in northern Florida which the Spanish sought to destroy, and British sea captains ventured into many inlets in a futile search for a Northwest Passage to the fabled riches of India.

The chief competitors for the area from Maine to Georgia that would ultimately become the original 13 United States were Spain, England, the Netherlands, and Sweden. English colonization, the first and in time foremost, was by royal charter divided between two companies: the Virginia

JAMESTOWN SETTLEMENT

Company of London received rights to the southern section, which included Chesapeake Bay, whereas the Plymouth Company based in Plymouth, England, had rights to the northern section, which included what eventually became New England.

The forests and waters of the New World were bounteous; the Indians lived on waterfowl and shorebirds that filled the skies as they migrated, deer and smaller game that roamed the forests, seafood that abounded in extensive waters, and crops raised in small gardens. The English settlers learned from the Indians how to plant unfamiliar crops and prepare new foods as they hacked out homes in the wilderness. These new settlements were fragile. Many of the settlers were ill or worn out when they arrived, and the wilderness was at times unforgiving. Food and other necessities were scarce, and diseases claimed many. Some settlers became discouraged and went home. Now and then, as more and more settlers arrived, some neighboring Indian tribes turned hostile and massacred the recent arrivals in attempts to eradicate their settlements.

Jamestown, the first British foothold after Sir Walter Raleigh's ill-fated attempts in North Carolina, took root in 1607. There, a determined band of settlers hung on through a host of natural and man-made disasters. A decade later, the Pilgrims faced the

same kind of struggle in New England. They showed the way for later settlements up and down the coast. Meanwhile, the Spanish were firmly entrenched in St. Augustine, Florida, having settled there at the end of the 16th century. The border between their empire and that of the British was determined in 1733 by Gen. James E. Oglethorpe's bold move into Georgia and his successful defense of his settlement on St. Simons Island.

THE DeBURGO AND PELLICER HOUSE, HISTORIC ST. AUGUSTINE

CASTILLO DE SAN MARCOS, HISTORIC ST. AUGUSTINE

(*Previous pages*) **The entire community of Plymouth, Massachusetts can be seen in an authentic recreation at Plimouth Plantation.**

Historic St. Augustine

The atmosphere was gay and buoyant on September 8, 1565. Artillery boomed salutes, trumpets sounded, and 600 soldiers and settlers bearing bright-colored banners followed Capt. (later Adm.) Pedro Menéndez de Avilés ashore to found the city of St. Augustine, Florida. Perhaps the city would have been better named for Mars, the god of war, than for a saint, since it seldom knew a peaceful moment as Menéndez sought to defend it against Indian uprisings while protecting the gold-laden Spanish galleons offshore.

Menéndez did not just make war as a defender, but also battled "with fire and blood" against French Protestants who tried to settle in northeast Florida, building Fort Caroline near Jacksonville. In a surprise attack by land, he took Fort Caroline and killed most of the inhabitants. Later, he executed so many surrendering French seamen at an inlet 14 miles south of St. Augustine that the place became known as Matanzas, or "Slaughters."

While Menéndez in his dispatches to King Philip II of Spain boasted of slaughtering numerous Protestants, he pointedly remarked that he did so in defense of "Your Majesty's provinces," since Spain claimed not only Florida but most of America's east coast as well. Despite Menéndez's efforts, however, Spain found it increasingly difficult to enforce the validity of its claim against the strong thrust of other European nations seeking to exploit the wealth of the New World. Indeed, the fighting which gave Menéndez his savage triumph over the French was only the first major clash of European powers struggling for control of North America.

Eventually, Menéndez and St. Augustine suffered retribution, as Jean Ribaut, one of the slain French leaders, predicted they would. Vengeful French forces recaptured and destroyed Fort Caroline (renamed Fort San Mateo by the Spanish) and hanged the survivors. They also tossed overboard Spanish

Lorenzo Gomez, who lived in this house in the Spanish Quarter, was a soldier, but also operated an importing business on the side.

Balconies along narrow St. George Street, in the heart of Historic St. Augustine, Florida, reflect a 1740s Spanish atmosphere.

sailors captured at sea. In the warfare that followed, St. Augustine was bombarded by French and British warships and was sacked three times: in 1586 by Britain's Sir Francis Drake, almost a century later by Jamaican pirates, and finally in 1792 by South Carolinians and Indians. In 1702, the British burned the city but were unable to capture the fortress named Castillo de San Marcos. The Spanish in turn failed to destroy the British colony under Gen. James E. Oglethorpe at Fort Frederica on St. Simons Island in Georgia. In addition to the clashes with rival European powers, natural disasters (fires, hurricanes, floods) and Indian rebellions caused the periodic destruction of St. Augustine. Epidemics of smallpox and yellow fever, as well as occasional famines, ravaged the population. Yet, each change of sovereignty brought an influx of new settlers: the Spanish ceded Florida to Britain in 1763, regained East Florida in 1783, and

finally sold it to the youthful, expansionist United States in 1819. On July 10, 1821, U.S. troops formally took possession of the city in a colorful military ceremony.

Considering St. Augustine's turbulent history, it is surprising that the city has survived to become the oldest continuously occupied European settlement in the United States. But it has. Further, more than 40 historic structures have been restored or reconstructed in various parts of downtown St. Augustine to reflect the city's successive phases of development: the first Spanish period (to 1763), the British period (1763–1783), the second Spanish period (1783–1821), and the early American period (after 1821). Eight of the structures are used as museums, ten as craft shops, five as businesses, and others as offices and private residences. In addition, a number of handsome homes remain from the more gentle Victorian period, as does the Old St. John's County Jail.

Restoration and reconstruction of St. Augustine has been going on intermittently since 1936, when the Carnegie Institution of Washington, D.C., and several individuals helped Mayor

is a natural limestone composite of marine shells and coral from nearby Anastasia Island.)

While the Historic St. Augustine Preservation Board and predecessor commissions took the lead, other organizations, individuals, and companies contributed to the integrity of the colonial area. The Llambias House was purchased in 1938 by the Carnegie Institution and deeded to the city; the St. Augustine Historical Society took it over in 1955. A small museum opened in the Arrivas House in 1961. It was subsequently leased for a shop and offices, but it retains its authentic floor plan, walls, and woodwork.

The 1740s atmosphere prevails at the Spanish Quarter on St. George Street, just south of the City Gates. Known as San Augustin Antiguo, this barrio was home in the 18th century to an established community of mixed nationalities and races, including *criollos*, or people of Spanish descent. Today, it provides a backdrop for women in long dresses and soldiers in tricorn hats and blue and red uniforms who re-create day-to-day life in a garrison town. There are also restored and reconstructed houses of wood, cochina, and tabby that once housed soldiers and merchants a decade or two before the Spanish ceded the city to the British. (Tabby is a mixture of oyster shells, lime, and sand or gravel.)

Perhaps the best-known home in the old city is the González–Álvarez House, commonly called the Oldest House and Museum. It was constructed soon after the British left bodies strewn all over the streets of the burning town in 1702, but the site has been continuously occupied by dwellings since the 1600s. The house, acquired in 1918 by the St. Augustine Historical Society, has had both Spanish and British owners, but is named for Tomás González y Hernández, an artilleryman at the Castillo de San Marcos, and Gerónimo Álvarez, who acquired it in the late 1700s and whose descendants lived there for almost a century.

Later eras in St. Augustine's history are covered by the José Peso de Burgo–Francisco Pellicer House, a reconstructed frame duplex representing the second Spanish period, and the Antonio de Mesa–Juan Sánchez House of the American period, where interpretive exhibits and a slide show explain the careful research and archeology undertaken by those who have sought to preserve historic St. Augustine.

Beyond the Spanish Quarter lies a national monument, the Castillo de San Marcos, which overlooks Matanzas River. Construction was started in 1672 after the city had been sacked by the British, who continued to pose a threat from Charleston, their new colony in the Carolinas. Although the fort was besieged on several occasions, it was never taken by force of arms. Miles away at the entrance to Matanzas Inlet is Fort Matanzas, a stone outpost completed by the Spanish in 1742 after the British laid siege to the Castillo and burned the city.

Research, archeological excavations, and development are ongoing in the historic district. Recent efforts by the Historic St. Augustine Preservation Board have sought to maintain the ambience of the Spanish period. They also have discovered three previously unknown colonial structures on Marine Street and Avenida Menéndez.

The Oldest House in St. Augustine, constructed more than 250 years ago in Spanish colonial style, is also known as the González-Álvarez House, after two early owners.

Walter B. Fraser fund a catalog of historic sites and develop a course of action for their preservation. Later, the city and state provided funds "to be used solely for the preservation, acquiring, restoration and maintenance of ancient landmarks, sites and records of antiquity." In 1970, the area once enclosed by wooden walls and still bordered by City Gates made of coquina was placed on the National Register of Historic Places. (Coquina

(*Opposite*) A costumed interpreter welcomes visitors to the Triay House, now the orientation center for St. Augustine's Spanish Quarter.

Jamestown Settlement

On April 26, 1607, three British ships entered Chesapeake Bay and began searching for a suitable site for a colony. George Percy, one of the settlers, was impressed by the "fair meadows and goodly tall trees with such fresh waters running through the woods," but fertile soil and freshwater springs were not the only concern of the settlers. They needed a defensible site. The Spanish were eager to keep the British out of North America. Moreover, earlier unsuccessful attempts by Sir Walter Raleigh to establish colonies had exposed the volatility of the Indians.

The settlers—104 men and boys—chose an island in the broad James River, separated from the Virginia mainland by marsh and known as Paspahegh to the Indians. Its waters were deep enough so that ships could be moored close to land, while its marshes on the mainland side made it easily defensible. The first permanent English settlement was named after the reigning British monarch, James I.

The settlers faced a hard life in an unfamiliar wilderness. Many were gentlemen unsuited to labor; others recruited from the lower classes were just as unfit, or unwilling, to work. When Capt. John Smith became governor, he established a "no work, no food" policy, but some of his successors complained that many settlers would rather starve than work. Even the rough carpenters, laborers, and others willing to work were unprepared for the hardships they encountered. Their poor physical condition on arrival, unfamiliar diseases such as malaria, periodic conflict with the Indians, lack of sanitary conditions, and brackish well water sharply reduced their ranks. Food sent from England sometimes rotted en route or in storage or was eaten by rats. Only 35 of the original 104 settlers survived the first seven months of the ordeal, a high mortality rate that would go even higher in later years. Percy, in a report as governor, attributed the high death rate to "cruell diseases, as Swellings, Fluxes, Burning fevers, and by Warres [with natives]. . . . But for the most part they died of meere famine."

The "Starving Time" of 1609/10 resulted partly from an Indian attempt to wreck the colony by a variety of means, including the destruction of the settlers' food. Indeed, they killed most of the settlement's 600 hogs, drove the deer away, refused to trade corn, and killed settlers who left the fort. Of the 390 colonists living at the settlement, "not past 60 men, women and children, most miserable and poor creatures" survived to the following May.

Jamestown Settlement, just off the scenic Colonial National Parkway south of Williamsburg, Virginia, re-creates the condition of the early colony in authentic and stark detail: daub-and-wattle houses inside a small log stockade, three small ships that served as a link to the mother country, and an Indian village which reflects the lifestyle of the Powhatan tribes at the time.

(*Opposite*) **Just as his ancestors did in the early 1600s, this fellow is using daub to repair the wall of his house at reconstructed James Fort in Jamestown, Virginia.**

(*Below*) **Chores, such as those performed by these costumed interpreters, kept the settlers at Jamestown, the first successful English colony in the New World, busy from sunrise to sunset.**

The 20-ton *Discovery* was the smallest of the three ships to carry the settlers from England to the Virginia colony.

ethnically diverse work force including Polish and Hungarian master glassmakers; that the first vessel (a Dutch warship) bearing African slaves arrived in 1619; that the early industrial ventures did not prove profitable, but that the abundance of rich land created an agricultural economy that suddenly took a prosperous turn. When John Rolfe introduced West Indian tobacco to replace the milder local variety, the colony had a cash crop prized in England.

At the Powhatan Indian Village, buckskin-clad interpreters demonstrate everyday tasks such as curing pottery in an open fire, grinding corn, and weaving baskets. Several huts made of bark or mat (called long houses) provide a glimpse into the living conditions of the Indians. One is decorated with a feather cape, worn by a chief or medicine man, which the Indians believed had protective powers.

Beyond the Indian village is James Fort, a re-creation of the three-cornered log structure raised by the settlers within a few weeks of their arrival and attacked by Indians before it was completed. Its unimposing appearance provides little indication of the great events that occurred there: the birth of the Commonwealth of Virginia and the United States, the introduction of representative government in the Western Hemisphere, and the first overseas expansion of the English-speaking peoples, presaging the British Commonwealth of Nations.

Eighteen daub-and-wattle structures inside the fort re-create the first homes and public buildings in what was to become the United States. The houses, with dirt floors, are furnished with simple handmade furniture and a few utensils brought over from Britain.

The humble beginnings of the nation also are evident at reconstructions of the storehouse, church, and guardhouse. A work ethic existed here: settlers are required to labor from 6 to 10 a.m. and 2 to 4 p.m. to build and repair structures, and to farm and handle other chores for the community. Each man was required to serve in the militia, and drill was held at 4 o'clock every afternoon. The church, where visitors today hear interpretations of the early struggles, embodied the religious nature of the colony: church attendance twice a day was mandatory. Rules of conduct, called *Lawes Divine, Morall and Martiall*, were codified here by 1611. Moreover, in this church, the first representative government in the New World met in 1619.

The three ships tied to a dock on the James River—full-scale representations of the 110-ton *Susan Constant*, 40-ton *Godspeed*, and 20-ton *Discovery*—seem much too small to have journeyed across the Atlantic Ocean. On board the *Discovery*, which carried 21 passengers and crew, a sailor-interpreter shows visitors the cramped conditions in which the first emigrants lived during a voyage that took nearly five months. Here, visitors can learn about shipboard activities under Capt. John Ratcliffe. On board the larger *Susan Constant*, which carried about 60 passengers, visitors will discover that settlers were regarded more as cargo than as passengers and were seldom allowed outside their cramped quarters except during island stops. Refuse and waste were passed in buckets to sailors on the decks for discharge overboard; the lack of sanitation, rationing of food, and close quarters were some reasons that the settlers arrived at Jamestown in poor physical condition.

The *Godspeed* sails occasionally on good-will missions. A new *Susan Constant* will be constructed on shipways within sight of the present vessel, starting in 1990. The hull of the first vessel has deteriorated beyond repair.

Opened in 1957 by the Commonwealth of Virginia under the name Jamestown Festival Park, the facility was the focal point of the state's observance of the 350th anniversary of the founding of the colony. The state's re-creation, now called Jamestown Settlement, supplements nearby Jamestown National Historical Park, situated on the settlement's actual site. Its ruins include the tower of the settlement's historic church and the foundations of a number of 17th-century houses, as well as other historic sites and memorials. There are also statues of the Indian princess Pocahontas and Capt. John Smith, heroes of the early period.

The commercial origins of Jamestown are introduced at the Jamestown Settlement museum, enlarged in 1989. There, one can learn of the early trials that almost led to abandonment of the colony, and of the fortuitous arrival of relief ships. There, too, one can learn about the settlement's women, the first of whom landed in 1608, with a large contingent (about 90) arriving in 1619. The museum also reveals that the United States' first indigenous industry was a glassworks, which employed an

Plimoth Plantation

Few events have touched the American psyche as much as the landing of the Pilgrim Fathers at Plymouth Rock. Their high-crowned hats, buckled shoes, and plain clothes have become a national symbol of America's forefathers; the Pilgrims are extolled in prose, verse, and art. Indeed, they are often incorrectly identified as the first English settlers in the United States.

Many of these intrepid pioneers were members of a Puritan sect known as Separatists. In 1620, they sailed from Plymouth, England, in search of religious freedom aboard the *Mayflower*, a merchant vessel formerly used in the wine trade with France and the fish trade with Norway. The complement stood at 102; during the 64-day voyage, one child, Oceanus Hopkins, was born and one of the passengers died. Their destination lay in the vicinity of present-day New York, but a storm caused them to land at Cape Cod in what we now call Massachusetts. Although this was not the site they had permission to settle, they decided to remain where God had sent them and, under the Mayflower Compact, agreed to create and conform to their own laws.

An autumn arrival left them little time to prepare for the winter, which was especially harsh; indeed, for a time, the very survival of the colony was in doubt. Despite assistance from the Wampanoag Indians, nearly half of the settlers died during the first winter. Only four of the married women survived the cold and hunger.

By 1621, however, they could be truly thankful for their new lives. Pleased with the abundance of wildfowl, deer, and fish and enjoying an adequate harvest which gave them "about a peck a week to a person" to face the winter, they feasted in thanksgiving to God. Indians, led by Sachem Massasoit, joined in. This was not the first American Thanksgiving, but the Plymouth event is symbolically important and set the style of later autumnal feasts. To the Pilgrims, Thanksgiving was not a secular event but a day of prayer and humble recognition of God's bounty. In 1777, during the uncertain days of the Revolutionary War, when the Continental Congress proclaimed the first national day of Thanksgiving, it stressed the solemnity of the occasion. So have later presidential proclamations.

The daily life of the Pilgrim settlement is meticulously recreated at Plimoth Plantation in Plymouth, Massachusetts. The 102-acre living history museum has three elements: the 1627 Pilgrim Village, the Wampanoag Indian Settlement, and the *Mayflower II*.

At the Pilgrim Village, which represents the colony that was successfully underway by 1627, a palisade encloses solid thatched-roof houses with vegetable gardens and wicker fences fronting dirt streets. Interpreters in early-17th-century clothing work at everyday tasks and discuss, in appropriate dialect, the political, social, religious, personal, and medical issues of the period. The black and white clothing of the inhabitants is enhanced by red ties and jackets, striped hatbands, blue dresses, and beige skirts and pants. The Pilgrims had no aversion to color, only to pretentiousness. There is a fort/meeting house which reminds visitors of the importance of religion to these devout folk, but there are also areas for entertainment and recreation. Women cook, bake, and sew; men cut wood, push

Mrs. Fear Allerton and her stepdaughter, Mary, pass a vegetable garden on the way to visit a friend.

wheelbarrows, and plant crops. A burly blacksmith pauses beside his red-hot forge to discuss the economic life of the community, while a sailor describes the difficult voyage from England to America.

Community events such as court days, funerals, and weddings are observed at regular intervals during the warm months. On Muster Day in September, an actor portraying Capt. Miles Standish leads the men of Plymouth Colony in drilling and arms demonstrations with swords, pikes, and muskets. Harvest Festival in October illustrates trade and alliance negotiations with the Dutch from New Amsterdam, as well as sports contests, militia exercises, and feasting.

The Wampanoag Indian Settlement represents the history and culture of the dominant Indian tribe in southeasten Massachusetts at the time of the Pilgrims' arrival. Interpreters wearing authentic loincloths, buckskin, jewelry, and blankets stand beside dome-shaped huts covered with woven reed mats or bark. At times, they grind corn, weave baskets, harvest gardens, or cook over outdoor pit fires. Some wear traditional tribal facial markings.

Three miles away, the *Mayflower II* is moored at the State Pier in Plymouth Harbor. The full-size replica of the ship which carried the Pilgrims to the new land has the specifications of a medium-size merchant vessel of the early 17th century. It is 106½ feet long, has a beam of 25½ feet, a draft of 13 feet, and weighs 108 tons. The vessel was constructed at Brixham, England, in 1955 and sailed across the Atlantic in 1957 under the command of Capt. Alan Villiers.

On board the *Mayflower II*, interpreters portraying crewmen and passengers discuss the 1620 voyage and the social and religious philosophies which the Pilgrims transplanted to the New World. Visitors may inspect the master's cabin, where Capt. Christopher Jones and his mates studied charts on the original voyage; the great cabin and steerage, which provided relatively comfortable quarters for some of the more prominent voyagers; the less commodious 'tween decks, where most of the settlers lived; and other features of the ship.

An exhibit on the dock provides additional information on the voyage and the people who undertook it. Nearby are Plymouth Rock—located at the site of the Pilgrims' actual landing and protected by a stately portico donated in 1920 by the Colonial Dames of America—and two waterfront houses representing early styles of colonial architecture.

The Plimoth Plantation living museum developed from the dream of one man, Henry Hornblower II, who sought a meaningful way of recalling the lifestyle and activities of the Pilgrims. In 1945, he obtained the first donation to acquire land and prepare plans for "a living museum . . . [to] show how the Pilgrims survived and what they accomplished during the early years." The intervening decades have seen steady progress toward that goal; since the first "somewhat fanciful" house was reconstructed in 1949, the project has slowly evolved through the use of mannequins and interpretive signs to its present state as a working village where, since 1978, the emphasis has been on showing-by-doing. Completion of a new Visitors Center in 1987 marked another expansion of the interpretive program.

The village cooper, Master John Alden, provided an essential craft for the early Massachusetts colony.

"Mistress Alice Bradford," wife of the governor of the Plimoth colony, reads a rare dispatch from England in period surroundings.

Although the early months in Plymoth, Massachusetts, proved difficult, the richness of the land soon enabled the devout colonists to set a bountiful table.

THE COOPER SHOP

The colonial era that began at Jamestown, Virginia, lasted more than 150 years. New settlers arrived at the settlement periodically, and soon the small fort was too small to hold the growing colony. Farmers cleared land farther and farther inland and planted crops. Land grants, or "hundreds," given by the Crown encouraged the colonists to spread out. So did the discovery of a cash crop, tobacco. The site of Middle Plantation was settled as early as 1633; by 1699, it consisted of a few houses and the College of William and Mary.

That same year, the State House at Jamestown burned. Legislators, recognizing the shift of population away from the coast, decided to move the capital inland to Middle Plantation, which was renamed Williamsburg in honor of King William III. The town

quickly became the center of Virginia colonial life. In a sense, it also became the principal colonial capital. The eyes of the other British colonies in North America were upon it. Laws passed there affected a vast territory whose ill-defined western boundary lay somewhere in the vicinity of the Mississippi

River. The quality of royal governors sent from England differed markedly, but a tradition of citizen participation in government already had been established and was jealously guarded by able men of politics and letters. The colony's leading export, tobacco, was a prized commodity throughout Europe.

Colonial Virginians regarded themselves as Englishmen, with all the rights and privileges established by law. Their opposition to the Crown in the 18th century was based on that supposition. For men like George Washington, Thomas Jefferson, and Patrick Henry, whose names as Revolutionary War leaders are now legendary, the break with the mother country did not come easily. Indeed, many of the planters along the James River near Williamsburg were staunch Tories, steadfast in their devotion to their British origins.

THE ROYAL COUNCIL CHAMBER, THE COLONIAL CAPITOL

Colonial Williamsburg

W here can you—in the same day—ride in an 18th-century carriage, talk to a college "dandy" on the street, eat in a tavern that would be familiar to Thomas Jefferson or George Washington, listen to the tunes that entertained America's forebears (on instruments which they played), witness the drill of colonial militia, and watch a silversmith make 18th-century-style jewelry and housewares?

Colonial Williamsburg, the quintessential colonial capital, does it all and more. The historic area, 173 acres in the heart of Williamsburg, is the living, breathing 18th-century reproduction conceived by the Rev. W. A. R. Goodwin in 1926. Mr. Goodwin, then rector of Bruton Parish Church, communicated to John

D. Rockefeller, Jr., his dream of preserving the historic Virginia capital. To Rockefeller the idea had "unique and irresistible appeal," and its fulfillment became a personal goal for the remainder of his life. The work has been aided by other family members and now continues under the Colonial Williamsburg Foundation.

By the time restoration began, many of the colonial treasures had been lost and the 88 remaining sites were barely recognizable. The first building to be restored, in 1931, was the

The twin symbols of the British Empire—the lion and the unicorn—adorn the entrance to the Governor's Palace at Colonial Williamsburg in Virginia.

Wren Building of the College of William and Mary, the oldest academic structure in continuous use in the United States. The Raleigh Tavern was rebuilt in 1932, and the centerpieces of the historic district, the Capitol and Governor's Palace, were reconstructed in 1934. The hallmark of Colonial Williamsburg is authenticity, with archeology and research invaluable tools in the process; key research instruments range from a map of the city drawn by a French officer during the Revolutionary War, which pinpoints the locations of buildings, to a sketch of the third floor of the Governor's Palace made by Thomas Jefferson while he was Virginia's chief executive.

Colonial Williamsburg does not idealize history; the foibles and evils of the colonial and Revolutionary War periods are exposed along with the noble and honorable aspects. The evils of slavery are recognized, as is the crude but humane (for its time) treatment of the mentally disturbed. The ribald musical and thespian tastes of the era are not overlooked either.

Duke of Gloucester Street, the focal point of the historic area, is undoubtedly one of the handsomest thoroughfares in America. Historic brick eminences—the Capitol at one end and the Wren Building at the other—close the ends of the street. Between them lie taverns, crafts shops, homes, and Bruton Parish Church. Visitors stroll the broad street the way their ancestors did, talking with college dandies, men in knee breeches and buckled shoes and women in long dresses. Eighteenth-

century fare is served by costumed waiters and waitresses in authentic surroundings, while in the shops wigmakers, bookbinders, apothecaries, and the like perform their daily tasks. Also on Duke of Gloucester Street is the town's armory, the octagonal red-brick Powder Magazine. This was the site of trouble in 1775, on the eve of the American Revolution, when an anxious royal governor, Lord Dunmore, surreptitiously removed the town's supply of gunpower. The armed citizen's militia swarmed into the streets and demanded the gunpowder's return. Now, polished muskets, bayonets, and other relics are displayed in the racks of the renovated Magazine.

The Georgian governor's mansion faces the Palace Green, a long parklike section of ground off Duke of Gloucester Street. This elegant residence, which also served as headquarters of the royal governor, so dismayed taxpayers that they derisively called it the "palace," a name which stuck. During the Revolutionary War, it was the home of Virginia Governors Patrick Henry and Thomas Jefferson. In 1780, a year after the capital was moved to Richmond, the mansion burned. Today, the Governor's Palace has been reconstructed on its original founda-

**The restored Colonial Capitol in Williamsburg was the site of
numerous power struggles between the appointed Royal Governor
and the elected House of Burgesses.**

Basketweaving is one of more than 30 crafts performed in the 18th-century manner at Colonial Williamsburg.

tion according to records kept by early occupants. The 10 acres of grounds include several lovely gardens and a boxwood maze, a popular 18th-century diversion.

Every four years, the Virginia legislature holds a memorial session at the restored Capitol to recognize the important events which took place there. The reconstructed, H-shaped building reflects the composition of Virginia's colonial government: one wing holds the chamber and committee rooms of the House of Burgesses; the other wing is divided between the General Courtroom and the chamber where the Royal Council met. The interpretation in this building, including reenactments of political debates, courtroom trials, and conversations with ordinary people, is among the best in Colonial Williamsburg.

Other buildings illustrate the lifestyles of a variety of classes of Williamsburg citizens. The home of George Wythe, a prominent attorney (with whom Thomas Jefferson studied) and a signer of the Declaration of Independence, was built around 1775. His red-brick house, which is situated on the west side of the Palace Green, is noted for its garden, which combines productive and ornamental plants around a bowling green edged with boxwood. Across the Palace Green is an example of an early middle-class home, the frame Brush–Everard House, built in 1717 by a gunsmith and first keeper of the town armory (Magazine). Farther up the Green, the Geddy House and foundry represent the lifestyle of a well-to-do craftsman of the era. Artisans at the Getty House create fine pieces of silver. Like craftsmen throughout the historic area, who are creating boots,

barrels, musical instruments, and other items, they use 200-year-old methods in authentic surroundings.

One of the newest reconstructions is the Public Hospital of 1773, whose exhibits portray crude 18th-century methods for treating mentally disturbed patients. The underground DeWitt Wallace Decorative Arts Gallery, which visitors enter through the hospital, houses more than 8000 pieces of furniture, ceramics, prints, maps, and costumes. Also located in the historic area is the Abby Aldrich Rockefeller Folk Art Center, with its well-known collection of naive American art.

In order to help visitors understand 18th-century life, Colonial Williamsburg sponsors more than 1000 interpretive events each year, including musket firing and milita drills, fife and drum corps parades, 18th-century plays, lectures, architectural scavenger hunts, and even reenacted witch trials. Perhaps most popular are the seasonal events, especially the Grand Illumination for the Christmas season and, for July 4, the 50-day Prelude to Independence, which salutes the original 13 states. Many of the public buildings, including the Governor's Palace, are used for evening programs. The soft light of candles deepens the colors of the ballroom at the Palace as they did when the mansion's residents and guests listened to the dulcet tones of the harpsichord.

Carters Grove Plantation, on the James River 8 miles southeast of Williamsburg, stands on an 80,000-acre tract originally granted by royal patent in 1619 as Martin's Hundred. The mansion, built by a grandson of the original plantation owner, Robert ("King") Carter, is one of the most handsome homes in Virginia.

THE BIRTH OF A NATION

The long and turbulent period prior to independence was marked by increasing political strain and economic friction between the colonies and the mother country. The early dependence of the colonists on Great Britain for protection against the European powers dwindled after the French and Indian War. In the peace treaty of 1763, Britain won from France all of Canada and the interior to the Mississippi River. Now there arose problems of how to pay for garrisoning these vast new possessions. Although two-way trade between Britain and the colonies remained significant, economic interests were diverging. Britain viewed America as an exploitable source of raw materials and revenues, and so sought to limit colonial access to outside markets. Colonial merchants frequently ignored constraining British regulations and engaged in a profitable trade with the Caribbean colonies, even resorting to smuggling on occasion.

A tradition of self-government was strong in the colonies. It had been established in the original charter of

ELFRETH'S ALLEY

(*OPPOSITE*) THE LIBERTY BELL

THE SECOND BANK OF THE UNITED STATES

Virginia and practiced in the other colonies as well. Colonials denounced taxes levied against them by a Parliament in which they lacked representatives and chafed under other laws imposed by Great Britain. A series of revenue acts and new restrictions turned protest and petition into open revolt. When a law was passed requiring a British tax stamp on all documents, bundles of these stamps were openly burned and distributors were roughed up. Samuel Adams of Boston spoke for many colonials when he declared: "If taxes are laid upon us in any shape without our having a legal representation where they are laid, are we not reduced from the character of free subjects to the miserable state of tributary slaves?" Although the measure was repealed, the subsequent Townshend Act placed duties on many goods imported by the Americans. A decision to grant a monopoly on all tea used in the colonies to the East India Company touched off a new wave of strident protest, as well as nonimportation agreements. In Boston, patriots disguised as Indians boarded three tea-laden ships on the night of December 16, 1773, and threw all the precious cargo into the harbor. Similar acts of resistance followed in other colonies. Citizens in Philadelphia, New York, and Charleston, South Carolina, for example, refused to let ships unload their tea.

In retaliation, early in 1774, Parliament passed a series of stringent measures designed to punish the Americans. Among them was a provision closing the Port of Boston until the East India Company and British customs were reimbursed for their losses. More troops were to be sent to the colonies and quartered at their expense.

The colonies were already informally linked by committees of correspondence. Now, the Massachusetts House of Representatives called on all the colonial legislatures to send delegates to Philadelphia. In September 1774, the First Continental Congress met there and petitioned the Crown for relief from all the "Intolerable Acts" restricting freedom. But matters went from bad to worse. By the time the Second Continental Congress hastily convened in Philadelphia in May 1775, armed clashes had already taken place at Lexington and Concord, Massachusetts.

ST. PETER'S CHURCH

Independence National Historical Park

PHILADELPHIA, PENNSYLVANIA

The diadem of national independence sites extends across the 13 original states and includes significant battlefields from the lakes of upstate New York to the swamps of South Carolina.

A different kind of battle was waged in Philadelphia, where the Second Continental Congress struggled with the demands of waging a war and resolving peacetime differences between states to put in place the American political system which has survived for more than 200 years. Independence National Historical Park in downtown Philadelphia is a tribute to the genius of those men who conceived, through compromise, such a vital and durable system. Its various sites bring to mind the sweep of political events that led to independence, brought a new nation into being, and saw it through its early years. In these buildings, the political philosophy and organizational framework of the 13 rebellious colonies and, later, the new nation were hammered out in debate and compromise by talented and strong-willed men.

The main area of the national park extends from Second to Sixth Streets and between Market and Walnut Streets. Each of the 13 historic sites in the area played its part in formulating the philosophical bases of the Revolution. The quest for freedom, representative government, justice under law, and religious tolerance, underscored by a firm belief in God, are recalled at various places in the historic area.

The two most important documents in American history, the Declaration of Independence (1776) and the Constitution of the United States (1787), both emanated from Independence Hall, built between 1732 and 1756 as the Pennsylvania State House. There, in the Assembly Room, the silver inkwell reminds us of the moment when congressional President John Hancock of Massachusetts boldly affixed his signature in large letters to the Declaration of Independence, followed by the other representatives of the 13 colonies. There, too, is the so-called Rising Sun chair from which George Washington presided over the Constitutional Convention, exerting a powerful moderating influence on the sometimes heated debates. The Assembly Room has been restored to its appearance when the Founding Fathers met there between 1775 and 1787 (during 1777, Congress was forced to abandon Philadelphia when the British occupied the city).

The Pennsylvania Supreme Court Chamber, the Governor's Council Chamber, and various meeting rooms have also been restored to their appearance during that period.

(*Opposite*) **Philadelphia's Independence Hall was the seat of the American government during most of the Revolutionary War and the place where the Constitution was drafted.**

(*Below*) **The Assembly Room, where the Continental Congress met, looks much as it did when elected representatives struggled with the affairs of nationhood.**

The Liberty Bell, which was rung to proclaim the Declaration of Independence and became famous for a crack which it developed later, used to hang from Independence Hall's belfry. Now it is housed in a glass pavilion across from Independence Hall where it can be viewed from the outside 24 hours a day. The pavilion is open during daylight hours.

Carpenters' Hall, where the First Continental Congress met in 1774, is still owned and operated by the Carpenters' Company and displays a collection of artifacts used by Congress. Congress Hall features the restored chambers of the U.S. Senate and House of Representatives, which met there from 1790 to 1800, when Philadelphia became the new nation's second capital (after New York). President Washington's second inauguration was held there in 1793, as was the inauguration of President John Adams in 1797.

The men who served in these governmental bodies were not bloodless. They enjoyed the conviviality of Philadelphia's taverns. These lighter moments can be recalled at reconstructed City Tavern, which still serves meals. The Founding Fathers also roomed among the townsfolk; Thomas Jefferson lived in the now reconstructed Graff House while writing the Declaration of Independence. President Washington lived in the handsome stone Deshler–Morris House in Germantown at various times between 1793 and 1794. It was also home to British commander Lt. Gen. Sir William Howe, who set up headquarters there after his retreat following the Battle of Germantown in 1777.

The park and nearby area also offer a compelling introduction to the lifestyle of Philadelphia's citizenry. The Bishop White House has been restored to represent an upper-class home of the Revolutionary War period, while the Betsy Ross House at 219 Arch Street, operated by the City of Philadelphia, preserves the site where the famed seamstress sewed the first American flag in 1776. The house is furnished in the manner of a middle-class artisan.

Philadelphia's most famous citizen of the Revolutionary era was, without doubt, Benjamin Franklin. Today, Franklin Court covers a block once owned by the sage, whose homespun sayings are almost as familiar as his role as a patriot. The exteriors of five Market Street houses have been restored to their appearance during Franklin's era, while a white frame structure, created by modern architect Robert Venturi, marks the spot where Franklin's house stood. Archeological exhibits, a working reproduction of a 1785 printing press, and other historical relics are located in the area.

Religion played an integral part in early American life, and the area includes a number of distinguished houses of worship. Among them is Christ Church, built between 1727 and 1754 on Second and Church Streets. Franklin is buried in its nearby cemetery, at Fifth and Arch.

Other sites, such as the First Bank of the United States (whose exterior has been restored but which is not open to the public) and the Greek revival Second Bank of the United States (now a portrait gallery) give visitors a glimpse into the economic side of early nationhood. The Army–Navy Museum, whose collection depicts the military's part in America's struggle for independence, is housed in a replica of an 18th-century home.

Adjacent to the national park's modern Visitors Center is a 120-foot bell tower. The Bicentennial Bell which hangs there was a gift of the people of Great Britain.

(Left) In this modest Philadelphia house, Betsy Ross, a Quaker seamstress, fashioned the first Stars and Stripes.

(Below) A row of structures on the site of Benjamin Franklin's home commemorate the sage's association with his adopted city, Philadelphia.

THE REVOLUTIONARY WAR

In Philadelphia, the Founding Fathers were trying to secure America's independence through political and economic means, but the new nation's freedom had to be won on the field of battle as well. The first clashes of arms at Lexington and Concord, Massachusetts, were followed by eight years of warfare in which American hopes rose and fell with victory and defeat.

The commander-in-chief of the Continental Army, Gen. George Washington, was a veteran officer of the French and Indian War and was thus well aware of Britain's military might. He was a tenacious, resourceful combat officer. Though at times he took bold risks, he was basically interested in maintaining a credible force in good fighting trim, holding to the defensive when the British were stronger and wearing the enemy down through a series of harrying surprise attacks. Although he managed to force the British out of Boston, he could not dislodge them, given the strength of their fleet, from New York City and other coastal bases of operations. Nevertheless, he won the grudging admiration of British commanders, who called him the "Old Fox." After his withdrawal from New York, he explained his strategy to Congress thus: "We should on all occasions avoid a general action, or put anything

to risque, unless compelled by a necessity, into which we ought never to be drawn."

For a time, the British expected the rebellion to subside as passions cooled and wartime shortages affected the colonists' morale. This benign attitude was replaced by a policy of divide and conquer. The British held onto strategic ports—New York, Charleston, Savannah—and from time to time ventured forth on inland campaigns designed to break the Americans' will to resist.

Basically, the war was fought on two fronts, one in the North and one in the South, but fighting was sporadic and widespread in both sectors. The British suffered a severe setback when Gen. John Burgoyne's army of invasion from Canada was surrounded, soundly defeated, and forced to surrender at Saratoga, New York, in October 1777. This major American victory encouraged France, till then hesitant, to openly aid the rebels. Four years later, on October 19, 1781, Lord Cornwallis surrendered at Yorktown after being trapped by Washington's army and the French fleet. Both sides knew that British Prime Minister Lord North was correct when he exclaimed: "Oh God! It is all over!"

The martial side of the American Revolution is memorialized at a string of national parks in South Carolina, North Carolina, Virginia, Pennsylvania, New York, and Massachusetts. These are supplemented by an array of state parks and memorials. Together, Fort Ticonderoga, Hubbardton, and Saratoga battlefields typify the back-and-forth campaigning that dominated the struggle near the Canadian border. By contrast, Valley Forge and New Windsor Cantonment re-create encampments where the Continental Army wintered and trained.

VALLEY FORGE NATIONAL HISTORICAL PARK

Local re-created units of volunteers stretch from Canada and Maine to California. Many of these groups are tied together by umbrella organizations such as the Brigade of the American Revolution, which has almost 2000 members. Men and women in these units attend courses of instruction to ensure that their clothing, campsites, drill, weapons, and tactics are authentic. As many as 50 to 60 reenactments, tactical demonstrations, or encampments take place on weekends during the April–October period on the east coast alone. Special winter programs have been held at Princeton, New Jersey, and Fort Stanwix, New York. In Los Angeles, units demonstrate American and British camp life and 18th-century tactics once a month in a local park.

NEW WINDSOR CANTONMENT

SARATOGA NATIONAL HISTORICAL PARK

Fort Ticonderoga

Fort Ticonderoga, built by the French in 1755 on Lake Champlain at the New York–Vermont border, has all the qualities of a military bastion. It holds the high ground, controlling the water approach to Canada by way of Lakes George and Champlain. It is solid and imposing, seemingly impregnable. Despite its appearance, it was attacked six times and captured on three occasions: by the British in 1759; by the American rebels in 1775; and again by the British in 1777.

At the outbreak of the Revolutionary War, the fort became an early strategic objective of the Continental forces, who regarded it as a key point in blocking British operations into the United States from Canada. A bloodless attack by Col. Ethan Allen and his Green Mountain Boys captured the fort in 1775. Later, the able Gen. Benedict Arnold, not yet a turncoat, constructed and assembled a defensive fleet on Lake Champlain, but it was defeated by the British.

On July 6, 1777, after a four-day siege, British Gen. John Burgoyne captured the fort during his ill-fated campaign from Canada.

The fort and ancillary fortifications at Mount Defiance, Mount Independence, and Mount Hope demonstrate an important aspect of 18th-century military strategy—fortress warfare. Mount Defiance, a mile from the fort, has an even more commanding view of the lake than does Fort Ticonderoga, which it dominates; Burgoyne's troops forced the American defenders to surrender the fort by hauling cannon to the peak. The block-house at Mount Hope, about half a mile from the fort, was positioned to stop portage around the rapids between Lake Champlain and Lake George. The British abandoned Fort Ticonderoga and burned it when they marched south.

The fort and adjacent lands were acquired by William Ferris Pell in 1830; in 1908, one of his descendants began restoration of the fort according to the original French plans. Among the first historic sites in the nation to be restored, it is now a national park.

During the summer months, the gray rock walls of Fort Ticonderoga come alive with the shouts and smells of late-18th-century battle. Fife and drum units parade, while cannons fire at imaginary enemy ships on the lake. Although some of the presentation predates the Revolutionary War—France's successful defense of the fort in 1755 is marked, for example—the fort's museum claims to have the largest collection of colonial and Revolutionary War relics in the country. Displays include an exceptional assortment of swords, muskets, and pistols, as well as uniforms, engraved powder horns, paintings, and etchings.

In the nearby community of the same name, a replica of John Hancock's home houses the antique furniture and Revolutionary mementoes of the Ticonderoga Historical Society.

A fife and drum unit parades to martial music at Ft. Ticonderoga.

Fifers like these "British Soldiers" played a key role in formal parades during the Revolutionary War period.

"Revolutionary War soldiers" smartly shoulder flintlocks at Fort Ticonderoga, a stone fort built in 1775 in upstate New York.

Saratoga National Historical Park

Curiously, the battlefield at Stillwater, New York, honors one of the heroes of the 1777 Battle of Saratoga without mentioning his name. There is a monument to him with reliefs of a boot (signifying his leg wound) and epaulets (his military genius), and the inscription details his bravery and skill as he rode through heavy crossfire to join the assault on the Breymann Redoubt. The hero was Benedict Arnold, who was promoted to major general after the battle; three years later he became a "nonperson" when he tried to betray the nation he had hitherto so ably defended.

Arnold was not the only hero of the day. At Saratoga, his commander, Gen. Horatio Gates, achieved one of the few American victories of the early period of the war and one that many historians view as decisive in that it led to the formation of the French-American alliance. Following the battle, he was championed by his admirers in the Continental Congress as a replacement for General Washington as commander-in-chief until he led an army to disaster in South Carolina in 1780. Another hero was Col. Thaddeus Kosciuszko, a Polish military engineer serving in the Continental Army, who had chosen the site on Bemis Heights and fortified it. Monuments identify places where these and other heroes influenced the battle's course on the rolling lands beside the Hudson River.

The clash began September 19 in the neat fields of John Freeman's farm, with Col. Daniel Morgan's Virginians firing on the British advance guard from the vicinity of a log cabin. Repeatedly, the British reformed their lines and charged with fixed bayonets, only to be halted by accurate fire from the Americans. The British faltered, but reinforcements arrived to create a stalemate. Short of ammunition as darkness approached, the Americans withdrew to their fortified line on Bemis Heights. The restored Neilson House on the heights, which can be visited at the battlefield park, looks much like it did when American officers used it as a headquarters.

Gen. John Burgoyne, commanding the British troops, dug in and awaited reinforcement by a force he hoped was moving north from New York City. He did not know that, instead, Gen. Sir William Howe had opted to move south through New Jersey and capture Philadelphia. When help had not appeared by October 7, Burgoyne's supply situation became critical. He tried once again to turn the American left, sending 1500 redcoats and Hessians in an assault line across the Barber wheatfield. When they were driven back with heavy casualties, the initiative shifted to the Americans, who penetrated the British defenses at Breymann's Redoubt. On October 8, Burgoyne ordered a retreat northward to his fortified camp on the heights at Saratoga, but was surrounded by a growing American force that eventually reached 20,000. On September 17, some 6000 of the 9000 British and Hessian troops who had left Canada surrendered, marching out of camp "with the honors of war" and the stacking of arms.

The fortifications hastily thrown up by both armies do not remain, but a 10-mile driving trail leads to 10 stops where exhibits, audio units, and walking paths unfold the drama of the battle. Details of the fighting are covered on walks conducted by park rangers. In the Visitors Center, an audio-visual presentation describes the historic "checkmate on the Hudson."

Members of reconstituted units re-create 18th-century military life at periodic encampments; one is invariably held near the battle's September anniversary. Soldiers drill and conduct musket practice, officers sign up recruits, medical practices are described, and cooks prepare meals.

On the centennial of the battle, in 1877, a Surrender Monument was unveiled and the need to preserve the battlefield was stressed. However, the site was not acquired until the 1920s, and it did not become a national monument until 1938. The Schuyler House in Schuylerville (historic Saratoga), country home of Gen. Philip Schuyler, who had extensive landholdings in the area, was donated in 1950.

A "British officer" forms his reactivated unit in ranks during a demonstration at the Saratoga battlefield in New York.

Valley Forge National Historical Park

The struggle of the small army of poorly trained, ill-equipped Americans against the armed might of the richest, most powerful nation on earth can perhaps best be seen as a fundamental test—to determine whether the citizens of the new republic had the will to persist against great odds or whether enormous sacrifice and deprivation would cool their ardor for independence. In that light, it is well to consider the encampment at Valley Forge, Pennsylvania. "Of all places associated with America's war for independence, none conveys more the impression of suffering, sacrifice and ultimate triumph," asserts a brochure on Valley Forge National Park in what is, indeed, no overstatement.

Looking back from the perspective of a comfortable homelife in an affluent society, it is difficult for most Americans to conceive the hardships that George Washington and his troops endured during the winter of 1777/78 at Valley Forge. The Continental Army, which Washington worked so hard to maintain as an effective force, reached its nadir here: the troops were ill-clad, some even without shoes in the snow; there was little fuel to keep them warm; and food was extremely scarce. Some 2000 men died of hunger, disease, and exposure to the severe cold. Although Washington often wrote to Congress pleading for relief, that body could not persuade the states to provide it. As the winter wore on, the army dwindled, for many men simply went home. Had these farmers and storekeepers stayed away, the harsh winter winds and snow might well have accomplished what a British army had been unable to do; but they straggled back as the temperature rose, enabling Washington and his chief drillmaster, Gen. Baron Friedrich von Steuben, one-time member of the crack Prussian General Staff, to begin the training that would mold the Continental Army into a formidable force.

Thus, Valley Forge ranks in importance alongside Yorktown in Virginia, where Washington and his French allies cornered British Lord Cornwallis and forced his surrender, and Saratoga, New York, where a humiliating defeat sapped British will to continue the war.

Memorials at the Valley Forge National Park in the peaceful rolling lands of central Pennsylvania honor the sacrifices the soldiers experienced that fateful winter. Reconstructed log huts and earthen fortifications re-create the primitive conditions under which they lived. In the stone house that served as Washington's headquarters are the tables where he studied maps, received reports, and conceived operations such as the bold Christmas attack on the Hessian winter encampment at Trenton, New Jersey, that buoyed the sagging spirits of American soldiers and civilians alike.

Washington Memorial Chapel and Carillon stands beside a museum operated by the Valley Forge Historical Society in which Washingtonian and colonial artifacts are displayed, along with period military equipment and patriotic symbols.

During the warm months at Valley Forge, rangers and volunteers portray soldiers and "camp followers" at the reconstructed huts where Gen. John Peter Gabriel Muhlenberg's brigade was bivouacked. Others lead a 2-mile walk along the historic Trace Road which provides an overview of the organization and appearance of Washington's camp.

Each year, in December, there is a reenactment of the encampment, with rangers acting as intermediaries between 18th-century reenactors and 20th-century visitors. In mid-June, reactivated units engage in the kind of drill that General von Steuben initiated to make the army a disciplined force.

At Valley Forge, the Continentals continued to muster at arms despite the harsh winter weather which depleted General George Washington's army.

Yorktown National Historical Park

In 1781, after repelling all forces that sought to block his sweep through the South, including a smashing victory over Gen. Horatio Gates at Camden, South Carolina, in August 1780, British Gen. Charles Lord Cornwallis marched into Yorktown, an important port on the York River. He expected the Royal Navy to guard the sea lanes and resupply him, or evacuate his forces if need be. Instead, he found himself trapped when confronted by General Washington, commanding the American forces, who had rapidly marched 400 miles from New York State with the Comte de Rochambeau, general of his French allies, to join another force under the Marquis de Lafayette in Virginia. The allied army of 16,000 now beseiged Yorktown by land, while a powerful French fleet under Adm. Comte de Grasse off the Virginia Capes blocked Cornwallis's escape route. His surrender, October 19, 1781, virtually ended hostilities.

This fateful period is re-created at federal and state historical parks and the buildings in Yorktown which witnessed the fighting.

Yorktown National Historical Park preserves and re-creates portions of the fortifications used by the two armies in the battle. A section of the British inner defense line, which in 1781 stretched for 1½ miles around Yorktown, abuts the Visitors Center. Other key positions on a 15-mile driving and walking tour include Redoubt No. 10, which the Americans led by Col. Alexander Hamilton stormed and overran with fixed bayonets; the site of Redoubt No. 9, assaulted and taken by the French force; the Moore House, built about 1725, where surrender negotiations were conducted; and Surrender Field, where on October 19, 1781, a sullen British army laid down its arms to the tune of "The World Turned Upside Down." Rangers lead guided tours of the British inner defense line and offer demonstrations, including the nonfiring operation of period cannon. Other demonstrations are conducted by costumed soldiers on an irregular basis.

In the battlefield Visitors Center, a below-deck walk-through of a Revolutionary warship is among the most innovative exhibits. The "Lafayette cannon" was identified in 1824 by the Revolutionary War hero as one that had been surrendered at Yorktown.

The state-operated Victory Center, dedicated in 1976 as part of Virginia's participation in the national bicentennial celebration, flies the flags of the original 13 colonies. Inside the museum, the thoughts and reactions of individuals to the war are re-created along "Liberty Street," a late-18th-century block. At an annual outdoor summer encampment, interpreters dressed as soldiers drill and fire muskets while their wives and "camp followers" prepare food, sharpen knives, and repair clothing. The living history program is part of the attempt to place the fighting at Yorktown within the context of the period.

Nine buildings in the town also commemorate the battle. Among them is the home of American Gen. Thomas Nelson, Jr., circa 1711, which is open to the public. There is also the Customshouse, built about 1721, which is owned by the Comte de Grasse Chapter of the Daughters of the American Revolution, and Grace Episcopal Church, built about 1697, whose native marl walls have survived use by the British as a powder magazine, partial burning in 1814, and damage by a nearby explosion during the Civil War.

The Victory Monument, an 80-foot column topped by a statue of the Goddess of Liberty, stands on a bluff beside the York River. On the waterfront is a cave reputedly used by Cornwallis as headquarters during allied artillery barrages, as well as a pier beside which are preserved the hulks of wrecked British warships.

A reactivated American Revolutionary War unit demonstrates a charge at the Yorktown Battlefield in Virginia, where the surrender of the British forces assured America's independence.

**Drummers in 18th-century British uniforms beat out a command
at the Yorktown National Historical Park in Virginia.**

The Developing Nation

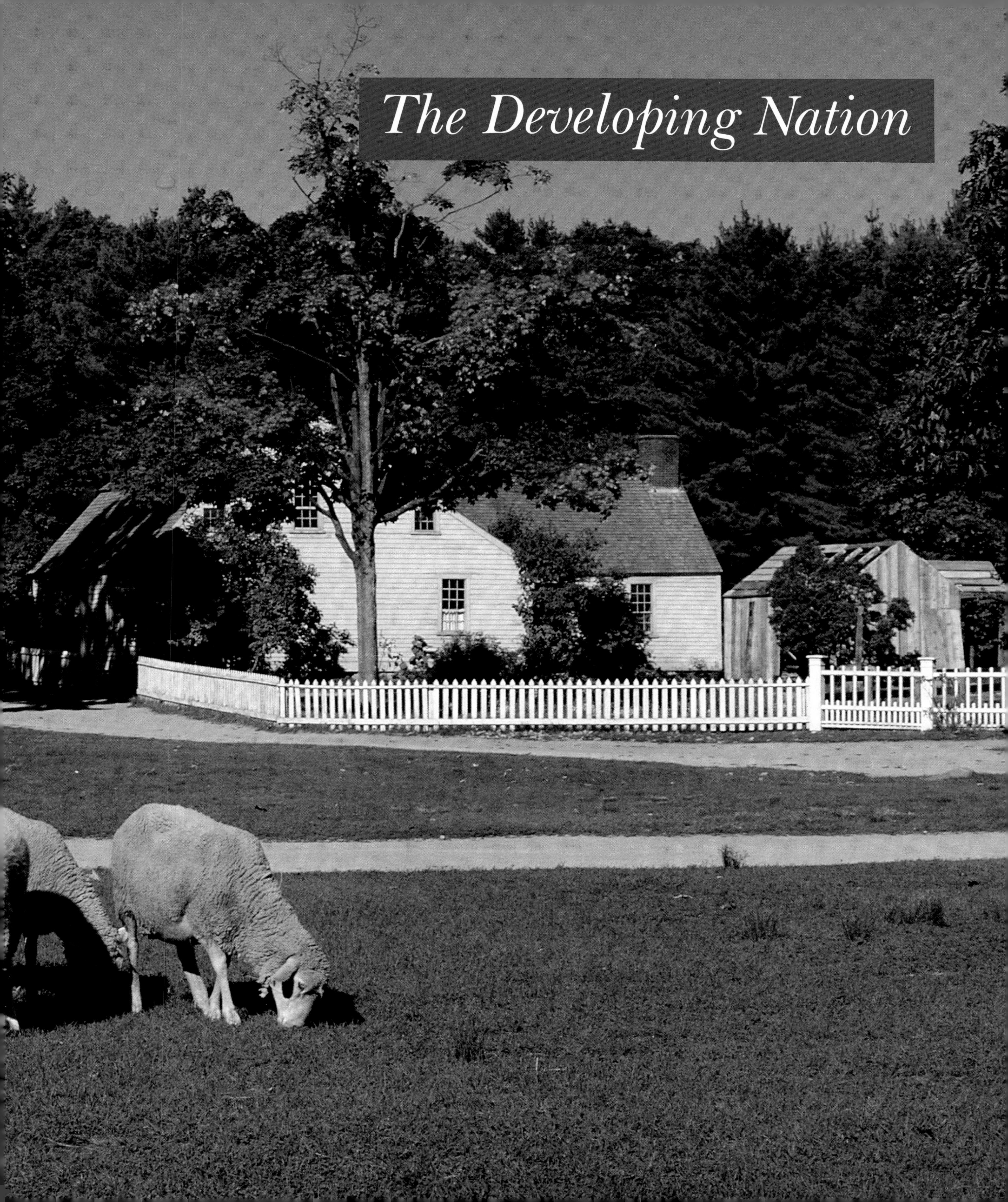

HANCOCK SHAKER VILLAGE

THE NORTHEAST

The optimism of the new United States was unbounded in the first half of the 19th century. The War of 1812 imposed only a brief restraint on an expansion whose roots lay in the previous century but which accelerated dramatically in the 1800s.

The first large-scale integrated cotton textile plant began operation in Waltham, Massachusetts, in 1816. Industrialization gradually expanded in the Northeast in the 1820s and 1830s. At first it was slow to take hold, but it quickly gathered momentum. Soon, machines were reducing the back-breaking work of farmers, and mass-produced goods were supplanting handcrafted objects. Machine-made candles, hardware, ceramics, and cloth allowed people more time for their own work—and perhaps even a little for leisure. Moreover, the developing network of factories provided new job opportunities, which in turn were an incentive for people to leave the

THE SHELBURNE MUSEUM

farms. The Northeast easily was the most productive region of the country by the 1850s. Still, industrialization was in its early stages; farming remained the largest occupation in the United States, and farmers had a major influence on state and national politics. (U.S. senators were then elected by the state legislatures, dominated by the rural vote.)

Already, the vitality that Alexis de Tocqueville discerned in *Democracy in America* was being felt in the arts as well. Perhaps the most telling—and surprising—aspect of this cultural apotheosis was the romantic belief that beauty and truth were inherent in commonplace things. This concept found ready acceptance in an impressionable country seeking to define itself and its destiny. More than that, Americans worked "with [their] own hands," as Ralph Waldo Emerson said, to produce objects of use and value to society. Art was less for art's sake than to fulfill practical needs (fine home-made furniture, weathervanes, patch-work quilts), portray the grandeur of

the American landscape (paintings of the Hudson River School), or record notable events (carvings and engravings). Even portraits by established artists tended to have a homespun quality, and so-called primitive art by untrained painters was often of remarkable worth.

The heritage left by this era is precious, and fortunately much of it has been saved by a nation not quite as eager to discard everything as de Tocqueville anticipated.

GENESEE COUNTRY MUSEUM

OLD STURBRIDGE VILLAGE

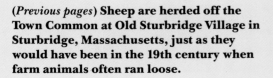

(*Previous pages*) **Sheep are herded off the Town Common at Old Sturbridge Village in Sturbridge, Massachusetts, just as they would have been in the 19th century when farm animals often ran loose.**

43

Old Sturbridge Village

At Old Sturbridge Village in Sturbridge, Massachusetts, restored buildings assembled from various sections of New England are united with reconstructions to re-create a slice of rural life during the 1830s. The village is typical of the thousands of orderly New England communities that existed in the region at the time.

Among the more than 40 buildings in the village are houses, shops, the elegantly columned Thompson Bank, a law office, and various industries and two meetinghouses, once home to religious congregations. Many of them surround a typical New England green. There is even a Town Pound, where livestock found running loose was held until claimed. A working farm, gardens, woods, and country paths on 200 acres of rolling landscape complete the museum complex.

Old Sturbridge is an outgrowth of the collection of brothers Albert B. and Joel C. Wells, executives at the American Optical Company. If Albert Wells had been able to play golf one rainy weekend in 1926, Old Sturbridge Village might not exist, at least not in its present form. But it was rainy, and Albert's friends persuaded him to join them on an antique hunt; thereafter, what he once regarded as "primitive" and "odd"—sausage makers, apple corers, rockers—became a passion. Soon, his home in Southbridge, Massachusetts, could not hold his collection of antiques; even converting his bowling alley and barns to storage and constructing additions to the house did not suffice. By 1935 the family moved into a new house in Sturbridge, and a year later the collection in their former home was opened to the public. Work began on a museum in Southbridge, but even this was not adequate. Finally, the idea of a village, a place where the objects could be displayed as they had been used, took hold. Old Sturbridge Village opened in 1946 and has been enlarged several times since.

There are six houses in the village, furnished as they might have been in the 1830s, to illustrate the lifestyles of different social strata within the community. For example, the 1796 white frame Towne House reflects the affluence of a village leader and prosperous farmer. By contrast, the less impressive Bixby House suggests the simple yet comfortable life of a blacksmith and his family, while the Richardson Parsonage, a 1748 "saltbox" house with a long, sloping rear roof, reflects the lifestyle of a

The rustic Freeman Farm typifies the rural atmosphere of 19th-century America.

A costumed interpreter
tends the flower garden
at the Towne House in
Old Sturbridge Village.

In early 19th-century communities, commercial and residential buildings rose in close proximity, as the Thompson Bank and the Fitch House at Old Sturbridge Village illustrate.

Congregational minister and his family (the Congregationalists were the dominant denomination in New England, but towns like Sturbridge also typically supported Baptist, Methodist, Episcopalian, and Universalist churches and the Society of Friends, commonly known as Quakers).

The level of technology prevalent in New England during the first quarter of the 19th century is demonstrated by an early-industrial sawmill, whose cast-iron "reaction" wheel, patented in 1830, is powered by water; a tin shop, just then beginning to appear in villages; a cooper's shop, which manufactured badly needed barrels for the community; and various other mills and shops.

The Asa Knight Store reflects the absorption of semiautonomous farms and villages into a national—and to some extent international—economy. The storekeeper was the factor, taking the products of the farm and village in exchange for manufactured goods from all over the world. This barter system allowed

farmers to purchase products that they would formerly have had to make and enabled tradesmen to specialize.

Seasonal cycles are observed at Old Sturbridge as they were in similar New England communities 150 years ago. This practice is most obvious at the Freeman Farm, typical of the 250 or so farms that would have clustered around a town like Sturbridge in the 1830s. In spring, straw-hatted men and boys prod oxen pulling antiquated plows in fields bordered by split rail fences. They shear sheep in May and June, toil with the hoe in the summer sun, cut hay with hand scythes and thresh grain in the autumn, and tap trees in late winter. Women's work is both seasonal—they cultivate a vegetable garden, raise herbs and flowers, and help harvest and dry food for the winter—and task-oriented—they cook pies and breads, spin and weave, make bonnets and brooms, and dye wool whenever time allows. Autumn and winter family activities include riding in horse-drawn sleds, maple sugaring, and cider making.

Elsewhere in the village, the blacksmith hammers red-hot iron into serviceable implements on his anvil, while other residents play period games, engage in storytelling, and sing old New England favorites. In July, they participate in an old-style Fourth of July celebration with a parade and the reading of the Declaration of Independence. They engage in drill, gun firing, and a mock battle on Militia Day, dig potatoes during Harvest Weekend, and make quaking plum pudding for a traditional Thanksgiving.

While many of the era's decorative arts are on view in village homes and shops, Old Sturbridge also maintains exhibition galleries which display folk art and New England clocks, as well as furnishings and artifacts that made homes more pleasant and moderated the hard life in an early-19th-century town.

Domesticated animals are cared for in the late 18th-century manner at Old Sturbridge Village's Towne House, the home of a prosperous Massachusetts farmer.

The tinsmith at Old Sturbridge Village uses 19th-century craftsmanship to fashion a milkpan.

Shelburne Museum

Electra Havemeyer Webb never abandoned her dolls. Indeed, the doll collection she began as a child, which reached 1000 pieces, sparked a life-long love for the handiwork of American carvers, metalsmiths, quiltmakers, and primitive painters. By the time she was 18, she had purchased her first cigar store Indian and, over the years, she continued to enlarge her collection of American folk and decorative arts. Her parents, Henry O. and Louisine Havemeyer, disapproved; they would have preferred that she join them in assembling one of America's greatest collections of Impressionist art, including paintings by Degas, Manet, and Monet (many of which are now in New York's Metropolitan Museum). Although Mrs. Webb acquired a few such art treasures, she reserved her greatest love for everyday things in which Americans expressed their feelings and love of form in the formative period of the nation's history. Ultimately, this pioneering collector of Americana scoured the countryside of New England in search of weathervanes, rocking horses, quilts, and other artifacts.

Part of her fascination with utilitarian objects was their uniqueness and beauty. Mrs. Webb's European experience with her parents and their adviser on art, painter Mary Cassatt, enhanced her appreciation of form and dimension, according to Robert Shaw, the Shelburne curator. Mrs. Webb's interpretation of folk art was a simple one; she said: "Since the word *folk* in America means all of us, folk art is that self-expression that has welled up from the hearts and hands of the people."

The Shelburne Museum is an example of a hobby that gradually became a passion. In forming her collection, Mrs. Webb did not set out to create a museum. That goal came later—in the 1940s—largely because of the need for a place to store her brother-in-law Vanderbilt Webb's collection of more than 130 priceless carriages and sleighs. Once she decided to create a museum, however, she approached the task with the same diligence and creativity with which she pursued her collecting. "To create something in arrangement and conception that had not been tried" was her explicit ambition. Historic old buildings, many in dilapidated condition, were purchased and moved to Shelburne. Some were transported intact; others were disassembled piece by piece and reassembled at the museum. Most required extensive restoration. By the mid-1950s, Mrs. Webb had purchased and relocated dozens of buildings and a 900-ton sidewheel steamboat. When the museum opened in 1952, it consisted of 11 buildings on 20 acres.

The museum as it stands today—37 buildings on 45 acres—is virtually a monument to the efforts of Electra Havemeyer Webb; by the time of her death in 1980, all of the historic buildings except one were in place. The more than 200,000 pieces of Americana form one of the most diverse collections of folk art in the world. At first glance, the museum appears to have no theme; it is, as one commentator observed, a "collection of collections." Actually, it has a very solid theme; it traces the development of New England life through the day-to-day implements which townspeople, tradesmen, and farmers used in work and play. Thus, it is in a sense a kaleidoscope of life during the years of the nation's greatest growth.

Most of the buildings are furnished in a style appropriate to the period of their construction, although a few serve as exhibition galleries. The Shaker Shed, for example, houses a collection of woodworking and craftsmen's tools, while the museum's nearly 1000 wildfowl decoys (the largest in the world) are displayed in the 1840 Greek revival Dorset house.

Many of the structures and objects at Shelburne provide insightful views into the nature of American life. For example, the A. Tuckaway General Store, moved to Shelburne in 1952, represents the state of American commerce before it was altered by specialization. Country stores such as this one not only served as a cozy meeting place for patrons, they also represented the primary contact that farmers and people in small communities had with goods and materials from other parts of the country. Therefore, storekeepers stocked as many household and personal items as space would allow. Every inch of the Tuckaway Store is filled with food, tools, clothing, and sundries, representing the actual stock of one Massachusetts general store. Hundreds of bottles of elixirs in the store's apothecary shop promise relief for everything from tired blood to sounds in the ears and illustrate the long-standing American passion for quick cures.

The Stencil House at Shelburne Museum owes its name to the attractive motifs which decorate the interior.

* The Shelburne Museum covers the period from the 18th century to the early 20th century. For a discussion of the museum's displays and activities pertaining to the latter half of the 19th century, see *Part V: The Maturing Nation, The Northeast.*

Several generations of 19th-century Americans received their educations in one-room schoolhouses like this 1830 example at Shelburne. It was customary for a number of grades to study simultaneously.

Vermont House, a 1½-story structure built in 1790, represents the home of a well-to-do sea captain, with 19th-century wallpaper stripped from a tavern in France and Waterford crystal from different periods selected by Electra Webb. In a way, the house typifies the American practice of improving and enlarging one's home as one's fortune improved. The builder, Asa R. Slocumb, continued to inhabit a log cabin while he constructed a new home around it. When the new home was closed in, he dismantled the cabin and carried the logs outside.

A cabin from Charlotte, Vermont, the home of a woodcutter, appealed to Mrs. Webb because of its simplicity and homemade qualities. Handcrafted objects on display inside include a rocking chair carved in 1860, toys, simple furniture, and a forerunner of the tricycle operated by hand cranks.

Also on view at the museum is a Jacquard loom, invented in 1790. This ingenious device made possible the creation of intricate designs in textiles through the use of punch cards, which created pre-programmed patterns. Thus, it is an early example of an automated system at work.

The one-room New England schoolhouse, built in 1830 by Gen. Samuel Strong and rented to the town of Vergennes, Vermont, for one kernel of corn per year, houses a patriotic wall hanging which, when viewed from different angles, changes from Presidents Andrew Jackson to Abraham Lincoln to Ulysses S. Grant. The school, where several classes studied simultaneously, was acquired in 1947 and moved piece by piece to Shelburne.

(Opposite) Shelburne's Tuckaway general store, circa 1840, was a social center as well as a merchandise outlet. Its shelves and counters abound with the inventory of an actual Massachusetts store.

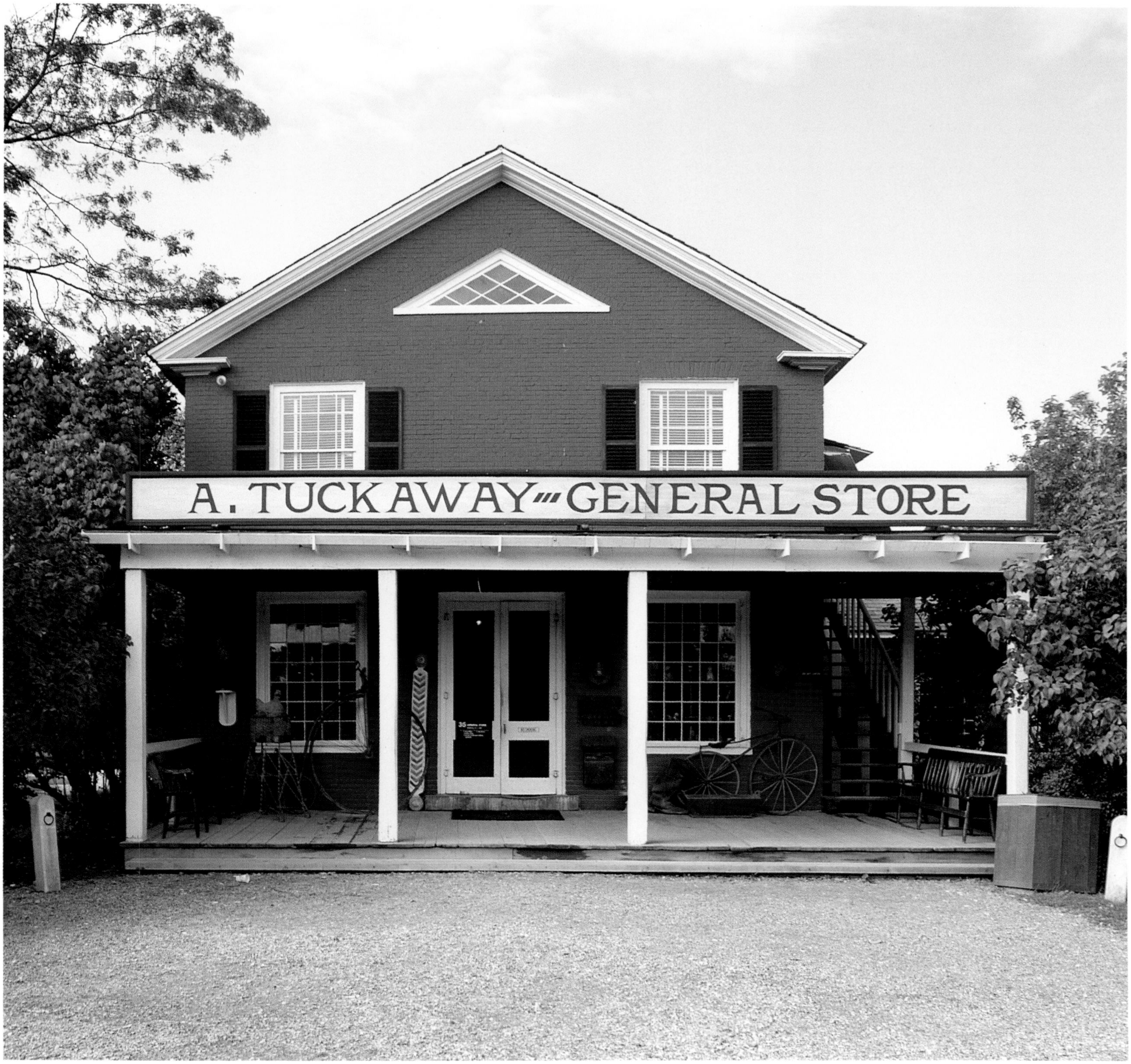
A. TUCKAWAY GENERAL STORE

"Spend a day in the 19th century," says a brochure introducing the Genesee Country Museum. More than 50 homes, farm buildings and shops in a peaceful valley near Rochester, New York, make up the complex which, indeed, evokes a feeling of nostalgia. The pace is different there. The "pleasant valley" (as Genesee means in the Iroquois language) was a productive farming region where the transition from log cabins to comfortable homes took only 25 years. The village stretches over a number of blocks and invites a casual stroll. Costumed interpreters act just as people did in varying decades of the 1800s. They tend herb, flower, and vegetable gardens, an essential aspect of life in the largely self-sufficient era of rural 19th-century America. They cook and bake, sew quilts, make baskets, fashion brooms, and weave and spin. They stop to give directions, and discuss the details of their daily routines. The brawny blacksmith hammers away in his shop. A bandstand in the Great Meadow beckons the residents to 19th-century-style entertainment.

The Genesee Country Museum is not only a journey through everyday American life during the 1800s, it is a treasure trove of 19th-century American architecture. For example, the first house moved to Genesee, the frame Amherst Humphrey House, built circa 1789 near an Indian path in Lima, New York, reflects simple frontier construction. A large central chimney heated the home's 10 rooms and served as the kitchen fireplace and oven. While Humphrey, like most pioneers, was basically self-sufficient, he depended on trade with the Indians and his neighbors to obtain certain commodities and utensils. He would have been very familiar with all aspects of trading posts, like Joseph Thompson's, circa 1807, located at the

museum. According to old account books, Thompson's stocked items such as nails, gunpowder, dyes, flour, tea, and coffee, which were given in exchange for hides, wheat, and other farm products. The 1½-story frame structure also served as a post office and provided lodging for travelers.

The white-columned Livingstone Manor, built in Rochester, New York, reflects the affluence that came to the region after the opening of the Erie Canal. Its first owner was entrepreneur James Livingstone, a member of an influential Hudson River family who made his fortune in milling, banking, and speculation. Built in about 1827, the Greek revival manor was one of the first grand mansions in Rochester's upscale Third Ward. Substantial modifications were made by Dr. Frederick Backus after he purchased the house in the mid-1830s. The Greek revival, or neoclassical, style was popular early in the 19th century because it was considered by many to be an expression of the democratic ideal. More than a dozen other examples of the style, dating from the 1840s and 1850s, may be spotted around the village.

Legends and stories are associated with many of Genesee's buildings. A case in point is what is now the bootmaker's shop. It was built about 1820 in East Avon, New York, as the office of a lawyer. One day, the lawyer rode out of town with a large sum of money; his horse found its way home, but the lawyer was never seen again. Nor was the money.

Other Genesee structures include an 1825 one-room country school and the 1855 Romulus Female Academy; a white frame physician's office, circa 1840; an insurance company, which the museum says is the "oldest insurance office in the United States"; and the stone and frame Enright Brewery, with

(*Right*) **The Romulus Female Academy, circa 1855, (***right***) was typical of the small private educational institutions established for girls during the 19th century. The Town Hall is at left.**

(*Opposite*) **Artisans fashion lanterns and other handsome objects at Genesee's tinsmith's shop.**

copper kettles and large wooden fermentation vats (this is the second reproduction of the brewery, based upon drawings made by a traveling Englishman in 1803). A large brewery wagon pulled by 12 horses is one of more than 40 carriages of varying styles and levels of quality housed in a carriage barn. There are also Methodist, Quaker, and Roman Catholic chapels and churches which illustrate the religious diversity of those who opened the valley.

Eight structures, including a one-room log cabin built in 1806 by Nicholas Hetchler, form a typical pioneer farm, where sheep graze in pastures divided by split log fences. While the one-room cabin is built of squared oak logs dovetailed at the corners, part of the wall around the fireplace is made of stone as a precaution against fire. Crude furniture in the cabin includes a wooden table and benches, a small bed, and straight-backed chairs.

The museum's reach extends well into the second half of the 19th century (the focus of *The Maturing Nation*, the final section of this volume). Among its principal holdings from this later period are the John Hamilton House, circa 1870, whose meandering walkway and shrub and flower plantings have been duplicated from an old photograph, and the Octagon House, circa 1870, which features a Gothic revival style with an Italianate cupola. It incorporates numerous interior innovations: water closets, water heaters, ventilators, hot air furnaces, and speaking tubes.

The making of Genesee Country Museum is a tale of determination, personal conservation, and community concern. Livingstone Manor, for example, was scheduled to be demolished in the 1950s but was saved by an admirer, who had it taken down piece by piece and stored until it was donated to the museum in 1970.

Children learn handicrafts in the shade of a tree outside the Red Schoolhouse, circa 1822, at the Genesee Country Museum.

**The Octagon House, circle 1870, was designed by a native of
Cohocton, New York, who claimed it contained more space than a
square structure of equivalent size.**

Hancock Shaker Village

The quest for religious freedom and the influence of religion on everyday life have been at the forefront of American activity since the nation's start. Each early settlement tended to be homogeneous; its citizens shared a common religion. But the steady influx of immigrants with diverse theological beliefs made freedom of worship an early and recurring issue. American independence brought great change; the separation of church and state was mandated by the Constitution. In addition, more and more sects, harassed or persecuted elsewhere, sought relief in the openness of American society and in the vast expanses of territory where few cared how others worshipped.

Hancock Shaker Village at Pittsfield, Massachusetts, owes its genesis nearly 200 years ago to such a religious group, one characterized by its preference for the simple things, its pursuit of an orderly, devout, and industrious life, and its belief that God was both father and mother of mankind and that, therefore, sexual relations were an act of self-indulgence. The group was the United Society of Believers, commonly called Shakers because of the way they moved at worship. They were the followers of Mother Ann Lee, a housewife from Manchester, England, an early exponent of equality of the sexes who introduced the movement to the United States. Ultimately, 18 Shaker settlements stretched from New England to Kentucky and the sect's adherents numbered perhaps as many as 10,000.

Hancock Village, the third Shaker community to be established, prospered at first through hard work and good fortune. The Church Families operated a gristmill, a carding and fulling mill which produced wool cloth for their own use and for sale, and a number of sawmills which provided lumber for building and woodworking. Occasionally, hired help was needed to supplement the labor of the Shakers. An iron ore deposit, discovered before 1810, was leased to a mine operator who employed 60 men to work it in 1853. They raised about 30 tons of iron ore a day by using a mule to haul buckets of the valuable ore up a shaft.

The village had 300 inhabitants at its peak in 1830, but its numbers dwindled as the years passed. So did other Shaker villages, including one in Pleasant Hill, Kentucky, which is also

(Opposite) This view of a room at the Brick Dwelling displays two types of furniture for which the Hancock Shakers were justly famous, rocking chairs and build-in wall chests.

(Below) This winter view of Hancock Shaker Village includes two of the village's principal farm buildings—the poultry house and the round barn.

More than 100 men and women lived in the 5-story Brick Dwelling, built in 1830, but the sexes were rigidly segregated.

now a historical museum. The decline is largely attributed to the sect's practice of celibacy. In fact, it is remarkable that the Shakers survived as long as they did. In their heyday, they perpetuated themselves by conversions and by adopting children and introducing them to the Shaker way of life. But the number of eligible youths diminished as private and public agencies created institutions for their care. Moreover, some children raised by the Shakers were lured away from the sect by the appeal of the outside world. Amazingly, though, it took until 1957 before the Shakers officially closed their rolls and ceased recruiting. Hancock Village was deeded to a nonprofit organization dedicated to preserving the Shaker heritage.

Today's visitors to the village can get a clear picture of the Shaker way of life and an appreciation for the sect's craftsmanship, which is highly regarded for its simple elegance. The Shakers professed a strong work ethic—"hands to work, hearts to God"—and believed that anything worth doing was worth doing well. Indeed, while primarily farmers, they forged a highly distinctive style, especially in making furniture that is characterized by neat, unadorned lines and a keen sense of proportion. Examples, displayed at the village, include solid wooden tables and benches, rocking chairs with tape seats, footstools, and spinning wheels. Their talents are evident in innovative features such as a sewing stand, circa 1830, with a two-way drawer, a system of built-in cupboard-drawers for storage, and commodes vented directly into chimneys to eliminate odors. They used button tilters on the legs of chairs to prevent wear

on floors and rugs. They also made numerous farm implements.

The 20 restored buildings show an equivalent level of quality, with their simple lines and harmonious use of varying building materials. The Shakers gave tender-loving care to these structures, repairing and maintaining them constantly and upgrading them from time to time. The village museum reflects that heritage. Restored buildings range from the 1793 Meeting House (relocated from Shirley, Massachusetts) where the Shakers practiced their dancing/quaking form of worship, to the 1826 stone-and-wood round barn admired by novelists Herman Melville and Nathaniel Hawthorne on a visit to the site. This impressive three-story structure, measuring 270 feet in circumference, was the center of the village's important dairy business. The village also comprises a laundry and machine shop; a large 1835 tannery; a bath house, heated by one of the early Shaker plate stoves; and a poultry house.

Separate Sisters' and Brethren's Shops attest to the Shakers' extreme segregation of the sexes. At the Sisters' Dairy and Weave Shop, erected as a one-story frame structure early in the 1800s and enlarged to two stories a few years later, interpreters use a dyeing frame and large cauldron to demonstrate the methods used by Shakers to process wool from their flocks and flax from their fields. In the 1795 Brethren's Shop are practiced many of the men's trades—cabinetmaking, the making of oval boxes, printing, tinsmithing, bookmaking, and so on.

The Trustee's House, which dates from 1830, was the home and office of the sect's deacon, who watched over the property and managed trade with outsiders. The rest of the Brothers and Sisters were housed in dwellings like the 1830 five-story Brick Dwelling House, with each sex having its own stairway and entrance.

Costumed interpreters provide insights into the daily routines of the community, known to the Shakers as the City of Peace. Traditional music is performed in the Meeting House. Gardens produce the herbs and flowers used in cooking and medicines, as well as seeds for sale. Candlelight programs feature traditional Shaker songs and readings. Horse-drawn sleighs operate in winter.

This Meeting House, moved to Hancock Shaker Village from Shirley, Massachusetts, is almost identical to the one that originally stood on the site.

**Herbs prized for their medicinal benefits were dried in this room
at Hancock Shaker Village.**

✥ THE MIDWEST ✥

Early in the 19th century, the Midwest was still basically frontier, but gradually, as the decades passed, the population increased and living conditions improved.

Canals such as the Ohio & Erie between Cleveland and Portsmouth, Ohio, and the Miami & Erie between Dayton and Cincinnati carried an increasing number of people into the hinterlands, where they cleared the land for farms, searched for minerals, and turned log outposts into towns. Canals also fostered a two-way mutually beneficial system of commerce: manufactured goods and essentials flowed west, while grain, furs, and raw materials moved east, where they were linked to the rest of the world by great sailing fleets. Land routes, nota-

LIVING HISTORY FARMS

LINCOLN'S NEW SALEM

bly the well-worn paths through the Appalachian Mountains, supplemented the rivers in the east–west traffic of goods, materials, and people.

The region's extensive system of rivers and lakes facilitated settlement of inland areas. Flatboat barges that the likes of Mike Fink propelled into the national folklore made journeys—sometimes routine, sometimes harrowing—through areas contested by Indians. They carried goods such as furs, timber, and grain to markets at Louisville, Kentucky; sometimes, the more adventurous even went as far as New Orleans. They returned with household items of pewter and stoneware and metal tools.

But before the century passed the half-way mark, water transport had began to wane as railroads slowly advanced into the region, providing a new overland link to eastern markets.

Life was simple and unadorned, and hard work produced a passable living. When time could be spared for social

activities, visiting among friends and relatives was common. Sportsmen made time for cock and dog fights, and the local tavern was a perennial hangout. Churches competed with "socials," picnics, and lectures by visiting dignitaries. Thus, by midcentury, civilization had a firm grip on America's heartland.

LINCOLN'S NEW SALEM

Living History Farms

Most settlers traveling westward by wagon were seeking land. Many were not farmers, and few realized the trials and hardships that awaited them as they cultivated their new property. Living History Farms, a 600-acre museum just west of Des Moines, Iowa, tells their saga and that of the Ioway Indians, who occupied the region when the settlers arrived from the East. In total, the museum includes four farms and a rural village from the second half of the 19th century.* Some structures stand on their original sites, whereas others have been relocated from elsewhere. Additional buildings have been reconstructed by using traditional methods. Tractor-drawn hay racks operate on a regular schedule to carry visitors between the sites.

The modern perception of the American Indians as nomad is only partially true. Many tribes created semipermanent camps, where they practiced agriculture. At the 1700s-style Ioway Indian village, a cooperative venture between Living History Farms and the Iowa Natural Heritage Foundation, garden plots of corn, beans, squash, and pumpkin grow near bark lodges (*nahaches*) which housed the tribe. The home life of the Indians is discernible from the implements on display: gardening tools and cooking utensils of stone and bone, handmade pottery, and drying racks.

* For a discussion of the museum's displays and activities pertaining to the latter half of the 19th century, see *Part V: The Maturing Nation, The Northeast.*

Costumed interpreters illustrate how Indians performed other tasks, such as stripping bark from ash and cottonwood trees to make their homes and sweat lodges; the gathering of nuts, berries, and roots; the weaving of cloth; the chipping of flint rocks to create sharp points for their arrows; and the tanning of hides.

By the 1850s, the land the Indians had farmed had long since been taken over by the white settlers and the Indians had retreated farther west. At the museum's pioneer farm of 1850, the life of those settlers is vividly re-created. Muscular razorback hogs (a breed long since replaced by domesticated types) grunt and wallow. Oxen, milk cattle, sheep, and workhorses graze in summer pastures enclosed by split rail fences. Wheat, barley, corn, and rye grow in the fields, and chickens scratch and peck in the barnyard.

The one-room log cabin with a loft and the log ancillary buildings, including a barn with a threshing floor, a smokehouse, and a corn crib, are typical of the primitive facilities that helped the region's first farmers survive winter snows, spring downpours, and summer heat. The root cellar—temperature-controlled by a layer of earth—stored the food that provided sustenance through the long winters. Many of these foodstuffs

A post-and-rider fence frames the homestead cabin at the 1850s Pioneer Farm, part of the Living History Farms complex in Des Moines, Iowa.

After butchering, a pig is rendered into parts, some of which are used immediately; the rest are preserved for the winter months.

came from a garden, enclosed by a stockade fence, which yielded potatoes, beans, and similar vegetables.

To make the re-creation more authentic, men in large straw hats and suspenders maintain the farmstead, using only the tools that were available in 1850. They and their "wives," also in period clothing, perform other chores demanded of a nearly self-sufficient farm: milking, butter churning, spinning, weaving, dyeing, flailing, winnowing, soap- and candlemaking, basketmaking, and open-hearth cooking. They entertain themselves and their visitors with dulcimer music.

In addition, there are crafts demonstrations and a display of patchwork quilts (the museum has an outstanding collection of 250 antique quilts) and a series of special crafts and music events at various times during the year. The first special event at the farms, the Grain Harvest Festival, was inaugurated in 1970, soon after the museum's opening; the old fashioned Independence Day celebration started in 1976. One-week summer camps give children an in-depth exposure to the history represented at the site.

Like the farmsteads it represents, Living History Farms has developed gradually. It owes its origins primarily to Dr. William G. Murray, a long-time university professor who ran for gover-

nor in the 1960s and conceived the idea of creating the farms. A site for the museum was purchased in 1969, and construction of the first display area, the Pioneer Farm, was started in 1970. The 1900 farmhouse, moved to the site, became the centerpiece of a new farmstead in 1975. The Ioway Indian Village was opened in 1982. The Church of the Land at the Walnut Hill Village, now a popular place for weddings (which end with a horse-drawn carriage ride), was erected in 1984, the same year the Solar Home opened; other significant additions were made in 1987 and 1988.

The colorful and informative complex has attracted a number of well-known dignitaries, including Pope John Paul II, who visited the village during his 1979 tour of the United States. It was placed on the National Register of Historic Places in 1973.

**A lamb gets personal attention from a costumed interpreter at the
1850s pioneer barn at Living History Farms. About 150 animals,
including horses, cows, hogs, and chickens, contribute to the
atmosphere of the open-air museum.**

Lincoln's New Salem

Fall sunlight warms a costumed interpreter in the doorway of Dr. Regnier's house at Lincoln's New Salem in New Salem, Illinois.

N ew Salem is the place where Abraham Lincoln, in his own words, ceased to be an "aimless piece of driftwood" and began a career that ultimately took him to the presidency of the United States. It is as unpretentious as the time in which Lincoln lived. Yet, when Abe arrived at the bustling county seat on a flatboat working the nearby rivers, New Salem seemed to him like the new Jerusalem.

Many Lincoln sites are preserved in the Midwest, including his birthplace in Kentucky and boyhood homes in Kentucky and Indiana and his home as a prosperous attorney in Springfield, Illinois, yet none conveys the essence of Lincoln's homespun personality better than this village of log cabins, where he lived for six years. Here, as a young adult, he chopped wood, clerked in a store, served as postmaster and deputy surveyor, became a captain of militia in the Black Hawk War, and first studied law.

Lincoln's New Salem has been re-created on the town's original site, which was purchased by the Old Salem Chautauqua Association and conveyed to the state in 1919. Only the Onstot Cooper Shop, circa 1835, is original; it was located by the Old Salem Lincoln League, one of the organizations involved in the authentic reconstruction of the town, and returned to its original foundations in 1922. Subsequent assistance in preserving the historic town site has come from many sources. Young men serving in the Civilian Conservation Corps (CCC) during the Depression years cut down timber in surrounding forests to build the Rutledge Cameron Saw and Grist Mill, the Hill Carding Mill, and several other museum structures. Subsequent additions, based on archeological studies, have re-created virtually the entire community that existed when Lincoln lived there.

The 12 log houses, 10 shops, a school, and a tavern are furnished with antiques from the 1830s, the era in which Lincoln was in residence. Some of the pieces, identifiable as the property of New Salem residents during the Lincoln years, were located and donated by the Chautauqua Society, along with decorations and personal effects. Numerous individuals contributed a wide range of artifacts.

Costumed interpreters bring to life the frontier personalities of Lincoln and his fellow townspeople, discussing everything from their personal "lives" to the oxen and other farm animals. They bake bread, dip candles, pedal a spinning wheel, and hammer metal on the blacksmith's anvil. Craftsmen work as they did in the 1830s, producing authentic replicas. The *Talisman*, a replica of a steamboat that operated on the Sangamon River during Lincoln's day, recalls an era in which America's waterways were a primary means of transporting goods and people. Historically based performances are given by a summer stock group six nights a week from mid-July through late August.

Lincoln first came to New Salem while working on Denton Offutt's flatboat. When the boat was delayed in the village in 1831, Offutt was so impressed by the community that he decided to open a store there. He put Lincoln in charge of it. Today, a re-creation of the Offutt Store allows us to imagine the young Lincoln as a clerk. In 1832, Abe went into business for himself by giving a promissory note to Rowan Herndon for Herndon's interest in the store. (Herndon was unhappy with partner William Berry because he also had an interest in

Abraham Lincoln entered the business world as part owner of the Berry-Lincoln store in New Salem.

another store.) The two buildings occupied by the Berry–Lincoln Store are both reconstructed.

The citizens of New Salem had surprisingly diverse backgrounds and interests, and Lincoln no doubt visited most of their homes and all of their businesses at one time or another. One home that he certainly knew was that of Jack H. Kelso, who shared a "dogtrot" duplex with his friend and brother-in-law, blacksmith Joshua Miller. According to Lincoln, Kelso was an adept "fisherman, hunter and philospher," and Abe benefited by his instruction in those pursuits. Other reconstructed homes include those of Isaac Gulihur, who, like Lincoln, was a native of Kentucky and a soldier in the Black Hawk War, and Martin Waddell, who made fur hats.

The re-created church/schoolhouse was originally built by the community in about 1828. Church services and Sunday school were conducted there. Typical of many rural schools of the time was the effective, if rudimentary, system of education. Students learned to read, write, and do sums by repetition during the week. The pupils paid 30 to 85 cents per month to their tutor, Mentor Graham, who moved to New Salem in 1826 and first taught lessons in a log cabin.

Among the re-created businesses familiar to Lincoln are the James Rutledge Tavern, operated by a settler from South

Carolina who, along with John Camron, founded the town; the William Clary Store, located in the "rough" end of town, where cockfights, gander pulls, and wrestling were commonplace; the carding mill and wool house, which was powered by two oxen; and the saw- and gristmill, which required a dam across the Sangamon River (now a pond because the river has changed its course over the years).

Mobility was a hallmark of frontier society; people often settled for a time and then moved on. Henry Onstot, a native of Kentucky, arrived in New Salem about 1803 and built a log home and cooper shop. He later operated the Rutledge Tavern before moving to Petersburg. Lincoln himself moved to Springfield, were he achieved prominence as a lawyer and congressman before becoming President. Isaac Burner, who also migrated from Kentucky to build a home with a sleeping loft and raise two children in New Salem, returned to Kentucky in 1836. In 1839, two years after Lincoln left, when the county seat was moved from New Salem to nearby Petersburg, the village began to decline.

The New Salem Museum, a stone structure outside the historic area, holds items belonging to village residents during the short period when the community boomed, as well as other antiques.

(*Right*) **Setting the hoops in barrels was a task that required skill and a strong arm, as this New Salem cooper demonstrates.**

(*Opposite*) **The bright autumn colors of Illinois enliven the Lukins and Ferguson log cabin at New Salem.**

A Nation Divided

FLOREWOOD RIVER PLANTATION

THE COTTON KINGDOM

In the first half of the 19th century, the United States was divided by the issue of slavery. While that "peculiar institution" had disappeared in the North, the Southern states clung to it, led largely by plantation owners who relied on it as a source of relatively inexpensive labor. For decades, a delicate balance of power was maintained between the two regions. Every time a free territory sought admission into the Union—Maine and California to name two—a territory permitting slavery had to be admitted as well.

North and South were divided almost as much by their diverging paths of economic development as by the running debate over slavery. From 1800 to 1860, the Northern states had increasingly embraced the Industrial Age: textile factories developed in New England, iron foundries were established in Pennsylvania, and the agricultural equipment industry expanded in the Midwest.

Several new inventions had a great impact on the divergence of agriculture in the North and South. In 1793, Eli Whitney invented the cotton gin, which separated the seed from the cotton mechanically, instead of by hand. Henceforth, cotton was "king." Spurred by demands from the British textile industry and later from New England, cotton production spread throughout the South at an unprecedented rate: in 1800, some 75,000 bales went to market; in 1859, when the Cotton Kingdom extended from South Carolina to Texas, a record 5.4 million bales were produced. On the eve of the Civil War, cotton constituted two-thirds of the nation's exports.

Meanwhile, Northern agriculture, especially wheat production in the Midwest, was becoming increasingly mechanized. Cyrus H. McCormick invented the horse-drawn, steel-tooth reaper in 1834, which took the place of five men with scythes. John Deere, an Illinois blacksmith, produced the first American steel plow in 1837. By the 1850s, mechanical threshers were also in use.

In contrast, the South continued to rely mainly on human beings for labor. The number of slaves increased from less than 1.2 million in 1808, when Congress stopped their importation, to 3.8 million in 1859. In some Gulf state counties, slaves made up three-quarters of the population.

While a few pioneer manufacturing companies began turning out textiles in the South, life below the Mason-Dixon line was primarily rural. The South imported many manufactured goods from Great Britain and other European countries, which were often cheaper than such goods produced in the United States. Southern politicians fought protective tariffs demanded by budding Northern industries, which wanted to keep out competitive products from abroad.

Despite all these differences, with the economy of both regions booming, the 1850s were an optimistic decade. More than 3 million immigrants arrived in the United States between 1844 and 1854, mainly from Ireland, Germany, and Scandinavia. The California gold strike of 1849 brought frenzied Easterners to the Pacific Coast in large numbers. The number of educational institutions increased significantly, many founded by religious denominations. Women were being educated in large numbers for the first time.

But the optimism ended suddenly as the 1860s opened. Abolitionist agitation became intolerable to the South, aided by the refusal of Northern congressmen, spearheaded by the free-soil Republicans, to permit the extension of slavery in the West. Southerners spoke increasingly of states' rights, including the right to nullify federal laws they deemed unconstitutional. In the halls of Congress and in Southern state legislatures, talk of secession from the Union became ever more ominous. In November 1860, when Abraham Lincoln, a former congressman from Illinois, was elected as the first Republican President, secession became inevitable.

(*Preceeding pages*) **A blanket of snow overlays Gettysburg National Military Park, where in the heat of summer in 1863 a Confederate invasion of the North was repulsed.**

WESTVILLE

Westville

It is always 1850 at Westville, a 57-acre living history museum in Lumpkin, Georgia. That is because the community never existed as a real town. It was assembled, piece by piece, from nearby counties to represent a preindustrial country town of the old Cotton Kingdom in the decade before the Civil War.

This does not mean that it lacks authenticity. A great deal of effort has gone into making Westville represent a west Georgia village, founded in the 1830s, with about two decades of growth. The town's ground plan is typical of the period, and the streets are named for Georgians who were well known in the mid-19th century, at least regionally. As visitors find Westville, growth has produced comfortable homes, churches, government buildings, and essential services such as blacksmith and shoemaker shops. Empty lots show that future development in town is anticipated, especially since the Macon–Columbus Railroad has reached as far as Fort Valley.

Costumed interpreters introduce visitors to typical mid-19th-century life in the 30 structures on the site. Cooks in long dresses covered with white aprons remove aromatic biscuits from an open hearth at the farmhouse and sweet-smelling gingerbread from a wood-fueled stove at the McDonald House, built in 1843 by a Scottish merchant. Quilters sew at the 1842 Grimes–Fagin House, typical of a middle-class home of the period, while spinners and weavers work side by side. Elsewhere, "townspeople" demonstrate the art of making candles, brooms, soap, natural dyes, and furniture—all in the manner of the mid-19th century. "Families" grow vegetables near their houses, some of which are to be dried or stored for winter use. Farmers plant cotton, sugar cane, and corn.

A muscular blacksmith fashions small nails or pounds out an iron band for a wagon wheel, while his neighbors make bricks and split shingles using tools and machines with odd-sounding names, such as pug mill and hardy. Work animals assist the farmers and tradespeople. A mule-drawn plow, for example, creates a wavy furrow in a field, while a horse-drawn farm wagon moves slowly along an unpaved street.

The West House, the first building on the site, was the home of the grandparents of Col. John Ward West, for whom the village is named. The collection of Colonel West—history professor and later president of North Georgia College at Dahlonega—was purchased by the village in the 1960s. It gave Westville a solid foundation on which to build. The acquisition included five buildings, one of the perhaps half a dozen antebellum cotton baling presses still in existence, and a variety of artifacts such as spinning wheels and looms. The first building was moved into place in 1968, others soon followed, and the complex opened to the public in 1970.

Many of the buildings are painted, a sign of growth and prosperity. Some of the homes double as shops or offices, a custom still common in the 1850s. Those of the wealthiest families have "fancy" furniture, commonly made of pine with a mahogany veneer. A case in point may be found in the 1840 Greek revival Moye House. It is a "petticoat mirror," which

The imposing Bryan-Worthington House in Westville, built in 1831, combines elements of the colonial and Federal architectural styles.

ladies wearing long dresses would have used to examine their hemlines. The beds of these affluent citizens had either straw or feather mattresses which rested on rope slats, tightened by "bed keys."

By contrast, the log, "dogtrot" Patterson–Marret Farmhouse is humbly furnished with homemade straw-filled mattresses, patchwork quilts, and simple wood furniture. It has a traveler's room, with an outside door that was left unlocked for weary passersby. There is also a copper whiskey still typical of a common, though possibly inessential, farm structure of the period. (It is presently inoperative.)

The town's school system is represented by the 1832 Stewart County Academy, which features typical textbooks of the period and is furnished with original benches, including a short bench which served as the recitation spot (from a similar school in Eufala). The 1850 Climax Presbyterian Church stands as witness to the town's spiritual life. It was one of the earliest churches in Lumpkin, serving the congregation for more than 120 years. There is also the Randall–Morton General Store, which features nailheads driven into the sills of all its windows as an early anti-burglary device; a pottery pug mill, where clay was prepared and fired in a wood-burning kiln; and a 19th-century millpond and dam.

Community life is represented by a variety of institutions at Westville, and trials are reenacted at the two-story frame Chattahoochee County Courthouse.

Special seasonal events enrich the village's program of daily activities. An annual fair, modeled after an antebellum tradition in the area, begins in late September and includes 14 days of harvesttime activities. Among them are cane grinding, syrup making, and taffy pulling. Other seasonal events include the planting of crops in May and a traditional Fourth of July celebration. Christmas is a month-long holiday with a different program each weekend. A yule log is cut and set ablaze the first weekend (the goal is to find the largest possible log since by tradition no work is done as long as it burns). The greens are set afire after Christmas to symbolize the closing of the old year and the advent of the new.

Several nearby but unrelated structures, including the Bedingfield Inn in Lumpkin, also represent the decades before the Civil War. The 1836 inn, fully restored and furnished with antiques by the Stewart County Historical Society, is maintained as a museum focusing on travel accommodations for the period.

The "citizens" of Westville, a re-created 1850s Georgia community, tend their lawns and chat across picket fences. The imposing Chattahoochee Court House is in the rear center.

Florewood River Plantation

Cotton was—and is—king at Florewood River Plantation near Greenwood in the Mississippi Delta. Florewood is in every way a working antebellum plantation, with 26 buildings on a 104-acre site. Interpreters wearing period clothing perform the chores that an active plantation of the period would have required. In the fields, cotton is planted and picked and cane is tended, cut, and made into molasses the old-fashioned way. In some of the "dependencies" (small buildings whose activities support the manor house), candles are dipped, pottery is turned, corn is ground into meal, and a blacksmith hammers out tools and utensils. Horses and mules share fenced pastures, while goats in the livestock shed can be fed by visitors.

The big house, the home of the planter's family, is easily the most imposing structure on the plantation. The large, two-story Greek revival frame mansion with front- and back-tiered porches and double-brick chimneys looks toward the Yazoo River. Many of the plantation homes in the Delta were designed by architects from England and France, a sign of the prosperity that prevailed in the region in the 1850s.

Florewood's well-tended lawn, growing a combination of imported and native flora, is also typical. So, too, are the formal garden, the vine-covered gazebo, and the separate kitchen. The latter is connected to the mansion by a covered walkway, sometimes called a whistle-walk because servants bearing hot dishes whistled to announce their presence as they entered the mansion. The kitchen is equipped with dozens of utensils from the period.

Inside the mansion, the "planter," dressed in clothing of the 1850s, or his "wife," in a fashionable long dress, welcome visitors and discuss the way they live and work. They point out the unusual qualities of the interior design, including a pink-hued parlor, as well as the rosewood furniture, coin silverware, and "poor people's" china.

Ancillary to the big house is the schoolhouse for the planter's children, which doubled as a church on Sunday. A "schoolteacher" demonstrates the instructional techniques of an era that used only writing slate, blackboards, and a few books to teach Latin, English, history, humanities, music, and manners. Other ancillary buildings include a laundry house; domestic servants' quarters furnished with rope-slatted beds and mattresses of straw or cornshuck; a sewing/loom room; and a pottery shop. The shop also housed a hospital room, where slaves who contracted malaria, yellow fever, or other illnesses were treated.

An expansive lawn provides the appropriate setting for the handsome main house at Florewood River Plantation, an antebellum Greek Revival structure.

(*Above*) **The cottage of the overseer, who managed day-to-day operations of the plantation, was a combination residence and office.**

(*Opposite*) **This skilled potter would have found plantation life a bit easier than that of the average fieldhand in Mississippi before the Civil War.**

The planter directed the work of the plantation from an office, sometimes located in the mansion, but housed at Florewood in a separate small wood building. Much of the work concerned crops, especially cash crops such as cotton, corn, sorghum, and peas. An orchard growing apples, pears, cherries, and other fruits was an essential adjunct, while a vegetable garden helped provision the manor table and feed the slaves.

The plantation has a variety of mills, including a mule-powered sorghum mill from which a sugary syrup then popular in the South was produced; a combination grist- and shinglemill powered by an 1860 box-bed steam engine; and a ginmill where a steam-operated machine removed seeds from raw cotton, which was later pressed into bales for shipment. There is also a smokehouse where meat was preserved; the house of the overseer (manager), furnished in typical period fashion; the driver's house, occupied by a slave responsible for waking other slaves to make sure they were ready for work; and a "double house" (duplex) with wood-burning fireplaces, where two slave families lived in humble surroundings.

The Cotton Museum in the Visitors Center presents a portrait of planter society, through restored equipment, exhibits, and audio-visual presentations. Here one learns of the significance of cotton in the economy of Mississippi, the South, and the world, as well as how levees protected the rich farmlands from flooding by the river and how slaves, directed by overseers, raised the cotton that went to market by water.

The plantation complex was reconstructed by the State of Mississippi after Leflore County acquired the site in 1972. Although it is an authentic antebellum plantation in every sense of the word, Florewood is a representation, not a re-creation of a plantation that once existed. The name, likewise, is an invention, although it comes, as did those of many plantations and towns in the South, from that of a prominent citizen. In this case, the name, selected in a statewide contest, honors Greenwood LeFleur, a friendly and respected Choctaw chief.

What would have happened to the cotton after it left Florewood? It would have been sent to Cotton Row in Greenwood, Mississippi, where auctions on Ram Cat Alley and Front Street composed the second largest cotton exchange in the United States. The area has been authentically renovated and maintained. Additional insight into the agriculture of the Delta region is provided at Cottonlandia, a museum tracing the evolution of farming from Indian efforts in 10,000 B.C. through the plantation era and beyond.

SOUTHERN COMMERCIAL CENTERS

Since they were among the first places settled in North America, the port cities of Charleston, South Carolina, and Savannah, Georgia, were social and commercial centers for their colonies long before the Revolutionary War. Indeed, they were established communities with elegant homes and cultural amenities at a time when most Americans were still clearing land and living in log cabins. But the expansion of international trade that occurred in the mid-19th century turned Charleston and Savannah into bustling ports of call for merchant ships of many nations. Here, cotton, tobacco, tar, and other bulk products flowed outward to the rest of the world, and manufactured goods from the North and foreign countries entered the United States. This far-ranging activity gave Charleston and Savannah a more cosmopolitan outlook than that of their more isolated neighbors. Their world embraced Europe, Africa, and the exotic Orient. Eager to hear gossip and news from other places, mer-

HISTORIC CHARLESTON

chants and planters talked with foreign captains on the docks and invited them to dine in their homes. Their newspapers regularly carried news from abroad. Their libraries contained books of national and international significance. Many of the furnishings in their houses came from Britain or France. Many of their citizens went abroad or sent their children to Europe to study.

These ports also had active intercourse with the large, thriving plantations in the nearby countryside and the smaller, less prosperous farms of the hinterlands. The owners of the lowland plantations had so much in common with their urban compatriots that they formed a single society. Cotton bound them together commercially; the production of this staple had become so profitable by the 1850s that South Carolinian and Georgian lowland planters were acquiring land as far away as Louisiana and Texas. Relations with the upland farmers were less inti-

mate but became closer as the railroads extended their tracks farther and farther inland. Ready access to the hinterlands created new sources for products such as lumber and granite.

As the largest ports on the southeastern seaboard, Charleston and Savannah were friendly rivals. Traditionally, Charleston was regarded as the more important and the more sophisticated of the two. It excelled in everything: its ties with Europe were stronger, its merchants were richer, its port was preferred by mariners, its population was larger, and its cultural heritage deeper. Because of this, Savannah sometimes looked at Charleston with envious and admiring eyes. Being second, Savannah tried harder—with substantial success. The mid-19th century was generally a time of prosperity for both cities and financial well-being influenced their outlook.

HISTORIC CHARLESTON

HISTORIC SAVANNAH

Historic Charleston

Once upon a time, a native of Charleston introduced his city as the place where the Ashley and Cooper Rivers flowed together to form the Atlantic Ocean. This slightly brash jest is typical of local humor, but Charlestonians, like Texans, can get away with a touch of braggadocio because of their city's great charm.

Today, the beauty of antebellum Charleston is carefully preserved in a historic district comprising more than 2000 buildings. In no city does the aura of the Old South influence the senses more. Fragrant wisteria, jasmine, and tea olive grow along cobblestone streets, while the aroma of fruits, vegetables, and flowers mingle at an open market. Cuisine that includes she-crab soup and oyster pie somehow seems more flavorful here, and the scent of history appears stronger. The history buff's footsteps have a little extra bounce along the Battery or White Point Gardens, where Civil War cannon still point toward Fort Sumter. With the mind's eye, such an afficionado no doubt can see, on nearby balconies and rooftops, elegantly dressed men and women watching with excitement as the bombardment of this Union bastion starts the Civil War (April 12/13, 1861).

Charleston was founded in 1670 as the first permanent settlement in the Carolinas. The Spanish did not welcome a British colony so close to their territory and scowled when the city prospered as an outlet for plantations raising rice and indigo. By the time of the Revolutionary War, Charleston was one of the most important ports in the colonies and, as such, was an early target of enemy action during the conflict. Charleston repulsed two British attacks before falling after a two-month siege. Patriots were incarcerated in the Provost Dungeon of the Exchange Building, which is still standing. Lord Cornwallis used the city as a base for his invasion of the Carolinas and Virginia. When he capitulated at Yorktown, his treatment at the hands of the Americans was influenced by the harsh terms he had imposed on the Charleston garrison.

The old section of Charleston has more than 2,000 historic structures. This is a section of South Battery Street.

The Joseph Manigault House, built in 1803 in the style of Britain's Robert Adams, is an outstanding example of neoclassical architecture.

In the Civil War, too, the city was a focal point of action. Since South Carolina was the first state to secede from the Union, Charleston was rightly viewed in the North as a center of the rebellion. It was attacked on several occasions during the war, and was finally evacuated by Confederate forces early in 1865 as Gen. William Tecumseh Sherman's Union army wheeled northward after reaching Savannah during its "march to the sea."

Charleston is a composite of the languid pace of low-country ways, the nostalgia of plantation life, and the historical imperatives of the Confederacy. It has one of the handsomest waterfronts on the east coast. Palmettos and live oaks grow in the sandy soil of White Point Gardens. Square low-country houses with long multiple front porches are typical of a historic district dominated architecturally by 18th- and early-19th-century influences. A horse-drawn carriage takes sightseeers past the large Confederate Monument, turns the corner to pass

deep "single" houses designed to circumvent British tax law, and on Catfish Row, which became the setting for *Porgy and Bess*.

There are also abundant remnants of Charleston's life as a port city and entrepôt, one filled with the sounds and sights of seamen, artisans, traders, and slaves. Today old warehouses where cotton, lumber, and tar were stored shelter restaurants, shops, and condominiums. A number of small inns also occupy historic structures. Among them are the Battery Carriage House, built in the 1840s; King's Courtyard Inn, which occupies an 1853 row of commercial buildings; and Sword Gate Inn, known for its Regency ballroom and distinctive iron gate.

Public buildings attest to Charleston's cosmopolitan character. The oldest of these structures, the Old Powder Magazine, circa 1713, and the 1801 City Hall, first used as a branch of the Bank of the United States, are now museums. The Old Slave Mart Museum displays slave trade artifacts and arts and crafts by African-Americans. Dock Street Theatre—one of the oldest in the United States—occupies the Old Planter's Hotel, built in

(*Left*) This handsome doorway leads to St. Matthews Lutheran Church, erected in 1828, one of Charleston's many historic houses of worship.

(Below) The old Scottish Chapel on Meeting Street represents one of the 138 religious denominations in Charleston.

the Edmonston–Alston House, circa 1828, which overlooks the Battery, and enters other streets paved with cobblestones that came to Charleston as ballast on sailing ships.

Two outstanding examples of the neoclassical style of architecture associated with Britain's Robert Adams are located in the 789-acre historic area. Joseph Manigault House, built in 1803, has high ceilings, pine floors, cypress mantels, decorative plaster, and a hidden stairway that connects the second and third floors. A freestanding spiral staircase is among the unusual features of the 1808 Nathaniel Russell House, whose oval drawing room, hand-carved woodwork, brass fixtures, and garden also are outstanding.

The 1772 Heyward–Washington House was the home of Thomas Heyward, Jr., a signer of the Declaration of Independence; the servants' quarters, carriage house, and detached kitchen provide further insight into the early lifestyle of the city. The Aiken–Rhett Mansion, circa 1817, retains some of the original furniture and wallpaper.

Of course, Charleston was not all fine mansions. Evidence of life among the working class may be found along pastel-colored Rainbow Row, on streets packed with one-room-wide,

Drayton Hall, built between 1738 and 1742, is an excellent example of Georgian palladian architecture.

1809. The state-operated Citadel, a military college which maintains its long-standing traditions, houses a museum that delineates the cadet corps' role in American history. Its extensive collection of Civil War memorabilia includes two original Confederate flags. Other standards, uniforms, weapons, and documents are located in the Confederate Museum.

Charleston's historic district has survived wars, fires, a devastating earthquake, and (in 1989) Hurricane Hugo, but has at times been sorely threatened by the intrusion of modern life (like gasoline stations and the wrecker's ball). The first or-

ganized effort to preserve the city's vintage structures came in 1920 when the Preservation Society of Charleston stopped the demolition of Manigault House. Other defensive moves prevented large city museums from stripping historic homes, including the Daniel Heyward House, built around 1770.

In 1931, Charleston became the first city in the United States to formally designate a portion of its city as a historic area. The district it created includes some 400 buildings in 23 blocks. Later extensions incorporated nearly half the peninsula on which the heart of the city is located, or more than 2000 buildings. Height restrictions are so strict that the tallest building is nine stories. In the 1970s and 1980s, the city government utilized federal funds to advance the restoration program.

Historic Savannah

From Chippewa Square in downtown Savannah, a statue of Gen. James E. Oglethorpe perpetually surveys the city he founded in 1733. Oglethorpe would be pleased with what has happened since. The town plan that he laid out, based on an orderly arrangement of squares, still dominates the historic area, while beyond it has emerged a city that would surely surprise him. Massive live oak and magnolia trees, towering over bushes and flowers, turn the squares into restful oases. An occasional horse-drawn carriage stirs up nostalgic reveries, but soon a stream of automobiles hauls the visitor back to the present.

Savannah, Georgia, is the quintessential born-again American city. The Revolutionary War and devastating fires in 1796 and 1820 destroyed most of the colonial structures that President George Washington saw when he visited in 1791. The city not only rose from the ashes, it became one of the leading commercial centers in the South. A branch of the Second Bank of the United States was opened here in the 1810s in the stucco Pink House, built in 1790. By the 1850s, Savannah's population of 15,000, substantial by national standards, enjoyed the benefits of waterworks and gaslights, but fanciers of flowers had to fence their yards to keep cows away. Homes featuring high porches (to avoid the mud and dust of the streets) became more and more elegant. The town even had its own row houses, inspired by a local citizen's visit to London, where such urban residences were fashionable. Forsythe Park, large and well planted, was laid out for all kinds of community activities. Newspapers flourished, literary magazines came and went, and fraternal, benevolent, and ethnic organizations abounded, including the 1857 Oglethorpe Club on Gaston Street.

From its early days, Savannah was a multiethnic city; many of its citizens in the 19th century hailed from elsewhere. They constructed and reconstructed churches of many denominations, among them Episcopalian, Baptist, Methodist, Presbyterian, and Roman Catholic.

Savannah's modern renaissance started at a low point for the city. Like other communities, its core area decayed as the city spread out and lifestyles changed. The elegant homes built in the tenderloin days of the 19th century deteriorated. Deserted houses were often vandalized. Some of the handsome squares were eliminated to facilitate the flow of automobile traffic. Early efforts to reverse the blight achieved meager results, but Savannah began lifting its bootstraps in earnest in 1954, when the Historic Savannah Foundation (HSF) was formed to prevent the impending destruction of the red-brick Isaiah Davenport House, considered the city's most outstanding Federal-style building. The foundation acquired the house, which was built in 1820 by a Rhode Island master builder who had moved to Savannah; it restored the elliptical staircase, interior hallway arch, delicate plasterwork, and garden. Now an exhibition building, the house is furnished with antiques, including fine carpets.

Emboldened by its success with the Davenport House, the foundation embarked upon a campaign to revive—house by house and step by step—the grandeur of its historic area. Today, the district measures 2½ square miles and encloses more than 1100 historically significant buildings. More than 800 have already been saved and restored through a combination of individual initiative and ingenuity, friendly persuasion, and

organizational clout. Savannah also protects other districts which are more modern, including remnants of the Victorian era, which produced another boom in construction.

Thanks to all of the preservationists—past and present— one can now stroll through the city's historic district and get a strong sense of the era when Savannah was a significant port and commercial center. Factors' Walk, whose revival was spearheaded by Mr. and Mrs. Mills B. Lane, vividly recalls the noisy, bustling antebellum port when cotton, rice, naval stores, and lumber were major exports. Warehouses named for the various cotton factors (brokers) with walls formed of oyster shells, gravel, broken stone, and brick rise from the river level to the top of a high bluff. Once filled with cash crops awaiting shipment, these warehouses today serve as quaint hotels, restaurants, and specialty shops.

Once Savannah's River Street echoed with the shouts and laughter of sailors and the commands of factors storing bales of cotton. Today its buildings are used for shops, restaurants, and a museum.

(*Left*) Historic homes line East Bryan Street in the northeast quadrant of Historic Savannah.

The cotton exchange, a pivotal commercial center in the 1800s when Savannah was a world-famous cotton port, is now the headquarters of the Freemasons.

Many of Savannah's historic buildings have been converted to modern uses. The Pink House is now a restaurant.

The affluence of the city in its heyday enabled merchants and shipping magnates to build elegant houses. Among them is the William Scarborough House, in the English Regency style, regarded as the "ultimate in townhouse design," with an atrium and third-floor skylight. It was erected in 1819 to a William Jay design for William Scarborough, a wealthy cotton tycoon. President James Monroe danced in the ballroom (the only one in a Savannah home at the time) and later participated in the dedication of the Independent Presbyterian Church during a visit in 1819. Scarborough lost his fortune when he helped to finance the inaugural voyage of the *Savannah*, the first transoceanic steamship, which failed to make a profit. For a while, the house was used by other family members, and then for about 90 years, starting in 1872, it was the West Broad Street School. It was restored in 1973 as a museum and headquarters of the HSF.

The Owens–Thomas House, another outstanding example of Regency architecture, with a columned porch, double entrance stairway, and arched second story windows, was designed by Jay for cotton merchant Richard Richardson. The Marquis de Lafayette spoke here from a side porch during his 1824/25 tour of the United States. Interior features include curved walls and doors, recessed arches, carved fireplaces, and a bridge in the upstairs hallway.

There are many ways to see historic Savannah. Walking and bus tours cover the major sites, horse-drawn carriages wind around some of the 21 squares, and riverboats provide a perspective from the waterside. Special-events days are particularly memorable. Perhaps the most colorful is the Celebration of Georgia Day on River Street each February 12, the date of the 13th colony's founding. It features historical programs, a colonial costume contest, crafts demonstrations, and a pageant. Christmas in Savannah is celebrated in typical 19th-century fashion and includes trees from around the world, in keeping with Savannah's heritage as a multiethnic city. The St. Patrick's Day parade is one of the largest in the nation.

A number of sites near Savannah also represent the antebellum period. Fort Pulaski, established as a national monument in 1924, was one of a string of forts built after the War of 1812 to defend the nation's coastline. During the Civil War, it guarded the Confederate city and was frequently bombarded by federal ships. Another stronghold, Old Fort Jackson, is still standing. Older than Pulaski, it protected the city during both the War of 1812 and the Civil War.

Georgia's colonial beginnings are evident at a number of sites near Savannah, including the ruins of Fort Frederica, General Oglethorpe's first settlement, and Wormsloe, one of the early plantations built by Noble Jones.

THE CIVIL WAR

Despite the prosperity of the 1840s and 1850s, fundamental differences continued to separate the North and South, in particular the question of states' rights and the morality of slavery. Moreover, economic issues, including the ongoing debate over the tariff, exacerbated the sectional disputes.

The most emotional issue was the one of slavery. Congressional equivocation did not help. The Missouri Compromise, whose purpose was to maintain a balance between slaveholding and free states, was never accepted by the abolitionists, who continued to agitate for a total end to the South's "peculiar institution." The Kansas–Nebraska Act of 1854, permitting new states to decide whether they would have slavery or not, effectively ended the compromise. Positions on the issue were hardened by militant abolitionists like John Brown, who with five of his sons was involved in the violent strife between "free-soilers" and proslavery forces in the Kansas Territory. In October 1859, Brown and others seized the U.S. Arsenal at Harper's Ferry, Virginia (now West Virginia), as part of a plan to foment a slave insurrection. The arsenal was retaken by troops under Col. Robert E. Lee. Two of Brown's sons were killed, and he was severely wounded. Later, after a trial in Charles Town, (West) Virginia, he was condemned to death and hanged.

The presidential election campaign of 1860 further fractured the nation. The Northern and Southern Democrats split into two parties: the former nominated Senator Stephen A. Douglas of Illinois; the latter, Vice President John C. Breckinridge of Tennessee.

To further complicate matters, the one-time Whigs of the border states, now calling themselves the Constitutional Union Party, nominated former Speaker John Bell, also of Tennessee. The Republicans nominated former Congressman Abraham Lincoln of

THE CONFEDERATE MONUMENT, SHILOH NATIONAL MILITARY PARK

Illinois. With only 39.2 percent of the popular vote but 180 out of 303 electoral votes, Lincoln was elected President. Throughout the campaign, the Southerners had warned that a Republican victory would mean the end of the Union. South Carolina seceded on December 20, 1860; six other Deep South states soon followed. Indecisive "lame-duck" President James Buchanan, a Northern Democrat, denounced secession but held that the central government could not coerce a state back into the Union. President-elect Abraham Lincoln disagreed. In his inaugural address, he stated his determination to use all the powers at his command in order to preserve the Union. His call for troops resulted in the secession of four more previously wavering states.

On April 12, 1861, Confederate forces began firing on Union-held Fort Sumter, which blocked the entrance to the harbor of Charleston, South Carolina. This precipitated a bitterly fought war which lasted four years. Although Virginia and Tennessee were the main

battle areas, numerous armed clashes ranged from Pennsylvania and Maryland in the East to Arizona and Texas in the West. The Civil War cost more American lives than any conflict before or since. At least half a million soldiers and sailors died; the civilian casualties, including deaths from war-related malnutrition and diseases, were staggering. The Northern naval blockade of the South caused great hardship.

The Civil War has left a deep imprint on the national consciousness. Its battles are still being fought, and not just in the countless books being written on the subject or in the classrooms of military schools. Every year, thousands of men in Confederate gray and Union blue file into camps, where they clean their rifles and march onto the fields to reenact dozens of battles on their original sites. They are members of "reactivated" Civil War units, named for the troops that participated in the conflict. As many as 20,000 people participate in more than 180 reenactments each year. Among the major events are those at Glorieta Pass in New Mexico in mid-August; New Market in Virginia's beautiful Shenandoah Valley each May; Bentonville, North Carolina, prelude to the surrender of the last major Confederate field army, in March; Vicksburg, the last Confederate Mississippi River bastion to fall, in July; Atlanta, in early September; and Perryville, Kentucky, the second weekend in October.

The annual Gettysburg encampment draws about 1200 participants. Living history demonstrations are held at every national battlefield park, but National Park Service policy usually prevents actual reenactments. Demonstrations range from the re-creation of the horrors of the prisoners-of-war camp at Andersonville, Georgia, to the cannon firing drill at Antietam in Maryland.

Manassas (Bull Run) National Battlefield Park

The First Battle of Manassas (or Bull Run, as the Northern press called it) occurred on July 21, 1861. It was the largest battle ever fought to that time in the Western Hemisphere. A year later, a second clash on the same terrain was even larger and bloodier.

Manassas (Bull Run) National Battlefield Park, 25 miles southwest of Washington, D.C., preserves the scene of the two battles, which were fought to control a transportation hub, Manassas Junction, located between the Union capital of Washington, D.C., and the Confederate capital at Richmond, Virginia. A combination of signs, audio stations, memorials, reconstructions, and strategically placed period cannon follow the progress of the battles.

The Park Service Visitors Center is located on Henry Hill. Here, too, is a large equestrian statue of Thomas J. Jackson, the famed Confederate general who earned the nickname "Stonewall" at this site. Few of the battlefield structures have survived; even the strategic stone bridge is a reconstruction, but three trails cover the two distinct phases of the first battle: (1) a Union flanking movement that forded the Bull Run stream to attack Matthews Hill during the morning; and (2) the seesaw afternoon of fighting on Henry Hill which gave birth to the "rebel yell," thenceforth a fixture throughout the war. The Confederate victory at First Manassas ended in the North's panicky flight toward Washington, with dispirited Union soldiers and civilians who had come to watch the battle all mingling on the dusty roads.

Second Manassas (or Second Bull Run) was an adjunct to Northern Gen. George B. McClelland's unsuccessful Peninsula Campaign. A number of places along U.S. Route 29 and State Routes 234 and 622 mark key features of the battle, where Union and Confederate forces reversed the battlelines of the first encounter. Trails lead to other battlelines, including the unfinished railroad grade, still partly visible, which Stonewall Jackson defended until Gen. Robert E. Lee's arrival with the main body of troops. Other prominent features include the Stone House, used as a hospital by both sides at different times; Groveton Confederate Cemetery, where only 40 of 200 casualties are identified; and Chinn Ridge.

Living history programs recapture some of the drama of the repeated and unsuccessful Union attacks on the Confederate defenses.

While the first monument to the Manassas battles was erected in 1865, preservation of the battlefield did not begin until the 20th century. Manassas Battlefield Confederate Park, Inc., and the Sons of Confederate Veterans purchased the 128-acre Henry Farm in 1922 and, 16 years later, conveyed it to the U.S. government. Later acquisitions, including the purchase of the 312-acre Brawner Farm in 1985, brought most of the two battlefields within the park's boundaries. In 1989, Congress decided to acquire the site where General Lee had his command post during Second Manassas.

The Robinson House, owned by a freed slave at the time of the Manassas fighting, survived the war but was later destroyed. This reconstruction was built in 1926.

Vicksburg National Military Park

The Confederates "won" at Vicksburg, Mississippi, in 1989. That was the year "reactivated" Union troops reenacted a May 19 assault against Confederate earthworks and were thrown back. The previous year, the final stage of the siege was portrayed, in which a few hours of firing were followed by negotiations and surrender.

Some aspect of the furious fighting at Vicksburg is reenacted every year at fortifications not included in the 1700-acre Vicksburg National Military Park. Units such as Stanford's Mississippi Battery fire their cannon, while infantry units man old trenches to meet the assault of waves of Union attackers. The annual reenactment is sponsored by the 1858 Old Court House Museum, where 10,000 artifacts are displayed.

The actual siege of Vicksburg was the culmination of a year of strenuous and bloody campaigning by the Union commander, Gen. Ulysses S. Grant, to take the Confederacy's last Mississippi River stronghold. After much effort, he maneuvered his troops and gunboats downriver below Vicksburg, then invaded its hinterlands and cut it off from all means of supply by land or water. When Vicksburg fell on July 4, 1863, the Confederacy was cleft in two and Lincoln could proclaim that "the Father of Waters again goes unvexed to the sea." Northern morale soared.

Reminders of the siege are found almost everywhere in and around Vicksburg. More than 1400 monuments are spotted among preserved fortifications along a 16-mile drive in Vicksburg National Military Park. Artillery batteries stand on their original sites, and memorials and statues identify forts, redans, lunettes, breastworks, and terrain features. The white, domed Illinois memorial is one of the most beautiful, while the Missouri monument commemorates sons who served in both armies. Stockade Redan, which still stands, guarded one of the roads into Vicksburg and was a focal point of Grant's assaults on May 19 and 22. Fort Hill, so formidable that no Union attack was ever made against it, provides an excellent view of the river and countryside. The white frame Shirley House, the only surviving wartime structure in the park, is restored to its 1863 appearance. The site where Grant and Confederate Gen. John C. Pemberton met to discuss surrender terms was the first place to be marked following the battle.

Exhibits in the Visitors Center and living history demonstrations show the military and human sides of the siege. A mockup of a cave decorated with sparse household furnishings illustrates how civilians living in Vicksburg sought to escape the Union bombardment. Cannonballs, carbines, swords, and a mockup of a Confederate hospital room also are on display. The important role of naval power in the siege and during the war in general is explored at a museum near the national cemetery.

Antebellum homes in the city of Vicksburg include Cedar Grove, damaged by warship bombardment during the siege, and the 1835 Balfour House, used as Union headquarters after the city's surrender.

During breaks in the fighting, soldiers relaxed as best they could—as these re-enactors at Vicksburg are doing.

Gettysburg National Military Park

The battle of Gettysburg was a watershed event in American history. The battle, which was fought July 1–3, 1863, halted the last Southern invasion of the North and ended for all time any hope that European powers would recognize the independence of the Confederacy. Yet, Gettysburg became a battlefield more by chance than by design. After his impressive victory at Chancellorsville against a vastly superior force, Lee invaded the North in an attempt to weaken Union morale, obtain supplies, and shift attention from Vicksburg, Mississippi, then under siege by Union forces under Gen. Ulysses S. Grant. Lee's army and that of Union Gen. George G. Meade, ordered to block the Confederate move north, collided fatefully at Gettysburg, Pennsylvania. Three days of bloody fighting ended with the renowned assault of Gen. George E. Pickett's Confederate troops against arrayed cannon and entrenched sharpshooters. Pickett's Charge has gone down in history as a symbol of Southern courage in the face of adversity, but it failed to break the center of the Union line. The totals for the three days of fighting were awesome: 27,000 dead for the North, and 25,000 for the South (American losses for the entire Vietnam War were 58,000). Lee, having lost one-third of his army, withdrew to Virginia on July 4, 1863. That same momentous day, Vicksburg fell.

Of all the Civil War battlefields, the one at Gettysburg is the best known and most visited. A drive-through tour along 40 miles of scenic roads follows the major landmarks of the battle. More than 1000 monuments and cannon identify sites such as the Angle (sometimes called the Bloody Angle) which overlooks the ground covered by Pickett's Charge; the Copse of Trees—a stand of chestnut oaks reached by only a few of Pickett's Confederates, who were then driven back by a fierce Union counterattack; the Wheatfield and Death Valley, where hundreds died in fighting prior to Pickett's Charge; and Confederate Avenue along Lee's battle line. One of the most impressive monuments on the battlefield is the Virginia Memorial near the center of the line, from which Lee, in great anguish, watched Pickett's Charge. The battle of Gettysburg also can be viewed in electric map and static display form at the Visitors Center, on a cyclorama housed in its own building, and from an observation tower. Aircraft carry visitors on regular flights over the 25 square miles of the battlefield.

Gettysburg National Cemetery is located near the Visitors Center. Lincoln's brief Gettysburg Address, heard by few at the time but now an American classic, is engraved on a memorial in the cemetery.

(*Opposite*) **Union General Gouveneur Kemble Warren is memorialized on Little Round Top, a strategically important site during the Battle of Gettysburg which the chief engineer of the army of the Potomac helped to save for the Union.**

(*Below*) **The Peach Orchard was the scene of an intense and bloody struggle on July 2, 1863 between the Confederate forces under Gen. James Lonstreet and the Union troops under Gen. Daniel E. Sickles.**

New Market Battlefield

The Shenandoah Valley of Virginia, the breadbasket of Gen. Robert E. Lee's Army of Northern Virginia, was a major Union objective throughout the Civil War. On numerous occasions, Union forces advanced down the valley in an effort to deprive Lee of this strategic resource. Most engagements ended, as did the Battle of New Market, Virginia, May 1864, in Confederate victory.

Each May, during the reenactment of the battle, smoke from brisk artillery fire at times obscures the sloping battlefield, where units are formed in ranks. A volley from the Confederates at the base of Bushong Hill draws fire from the blue-clad infantry and artillery holding the high ground. A Confederate advance begins, slowly at first and then rapidly into the Union lines. This charge is the final act in a vivid reenactment that starts with preliminary skirmishing near the present Hall of Valor museum, progresses across the rolling fields, past the Bushong farmhouse, through the "Field of Lost Shoes" (where mud sucked shoes off the attacking Confederates), and over split rail fences.

The annual reenactment on the weekend closest to the May 15 anniversary of the battle normally brings together more than 1000 men from about a dozen states, including those as far away as Arizona, California, and Michigan. The Sunday "battle" is preceded by an encampment that includes drilling, cooking, and other related activities. The nearby town of New Market sponsors "Heritage Days," including a parade in which the citizenry wear 1860s gowns and uniforms.

New Market Battlefield Park preserves 160 acres of the battle site. Bushong Hill, on which the main fighting took place, is arranged for a walking tour that includes authentic cannon on the high ground and an overlook with a fine view of the Shenandoah River and nearby countryside.

The Hall of Valor presents the battle in the larger context of the Civil War. Here, exhibits range from a Napoleon 12-pounder cannon manned by life-size mannequins to the personal effects of some of the men who took part in the fighting. Audio-visual presentations cover the battle and the legendary exploits of Gen. Thomas J. "Stonewall" Jackson, the Shenandoah Valley's favorite soldier.

A stained glass mural by Israeli artist Ami Shamir incorporates the names of the Virginia Military Institute cadets killed at New Market. These 247 "boy soldiers" had marched all night in the rain to reach the field of battle. "Put the boys in . . . and may God forgive me for the order," said Confederate Gen. (and former U.S. Vice President) John C. Breckinridge, hard pressed to find enough troops to halt the Union advance down the Shenandoah Valley. Taunted by the grizzled veterans as they moved into the line, the cadets were cheered by these same men when they captured a Union artillery battery at the crest of the hill.

Missouri veterans were the first to mark the battlefield. In 1905, J. H. Dwyer, who had been wounded four times in the battle, and W. R. Fallis, one of those who escaped injury, returned to place a large limestone marker that still exists. The battlefield was preserved by a 1911 VMI graduate, George Randall Collins, who purchased the farm in 1944 and left the site and an endowment to VMI in his will. The battlefield is on the National Register of Historic Places.

(*Above*) Union cannons are cloaked in smoke as they maintain a steady fire during a re-enactment of the Battle of New Market, originally fought in May 1864.

(*Opposite*) "Confederate troops" unleash a volley of fire during their assault up New Market's Bushong Hill in Virginia's beautiful Shenandoah Valley.

(*Right*) "Union soldiers" march to the battlefield at New Market, Virginia, where one of the largest re-enactments in the U.S. is held each May.

Appomattox Court House National Historical Park

The bloodshed of the Civil War did not end with the surrender of the Confederate Army of Northern Virginia at Appomattox Court House, but it was the beginning of the end. When Generals Lee and Grant, the chief commanders of the South and North, met at this crossroads village on Palm Sunday 1865 to discuss surrender terms, everyone knew that the war was over, even though some forces surrendered later.

Appomattox Court House National Historical Park re-creates the historic meeting of the two commanders in the McLean House, which has been reconstructed on its original foundations. (The original was taken apart after the war, exhibited, and then deteriorated in storage.) The reconstructed house is authentically restored inside, including the room where the signing of the surrender took place.

The village of Appomattox Court House looks much as it did in 1865. The reconstructed courthouse, which houses the Visitors Center, a museum, and a slide presentation, is the centerpiece of the restored village. More than a dozen structures stand nearby, including Clover Hill Tavern, the oldest surviving structure; the Kelly and Isbell houses, which depict two quite different lifestyles of the period; Meek's Store; and the Woodson law office. The Old Richmond–Lynchburg Road passes an area known as Surrender Triangle, where an audio-visual display re-creates the moving scene in which Confederate soldiers laid down their arms while their brethren from the North silently and somberly looked on.

(*Opposite*) **Generals Ulysses S. Grant and Robert E. Lee met in the McLean House at Appomattox to discuss surrender terms. The house is reconstructed.**

(*Below*) **The Isbell House at Appomattox has been restored to its appearance in 1865, when soldiers of the two armies lined up on nearby roads to effect the surrender.**

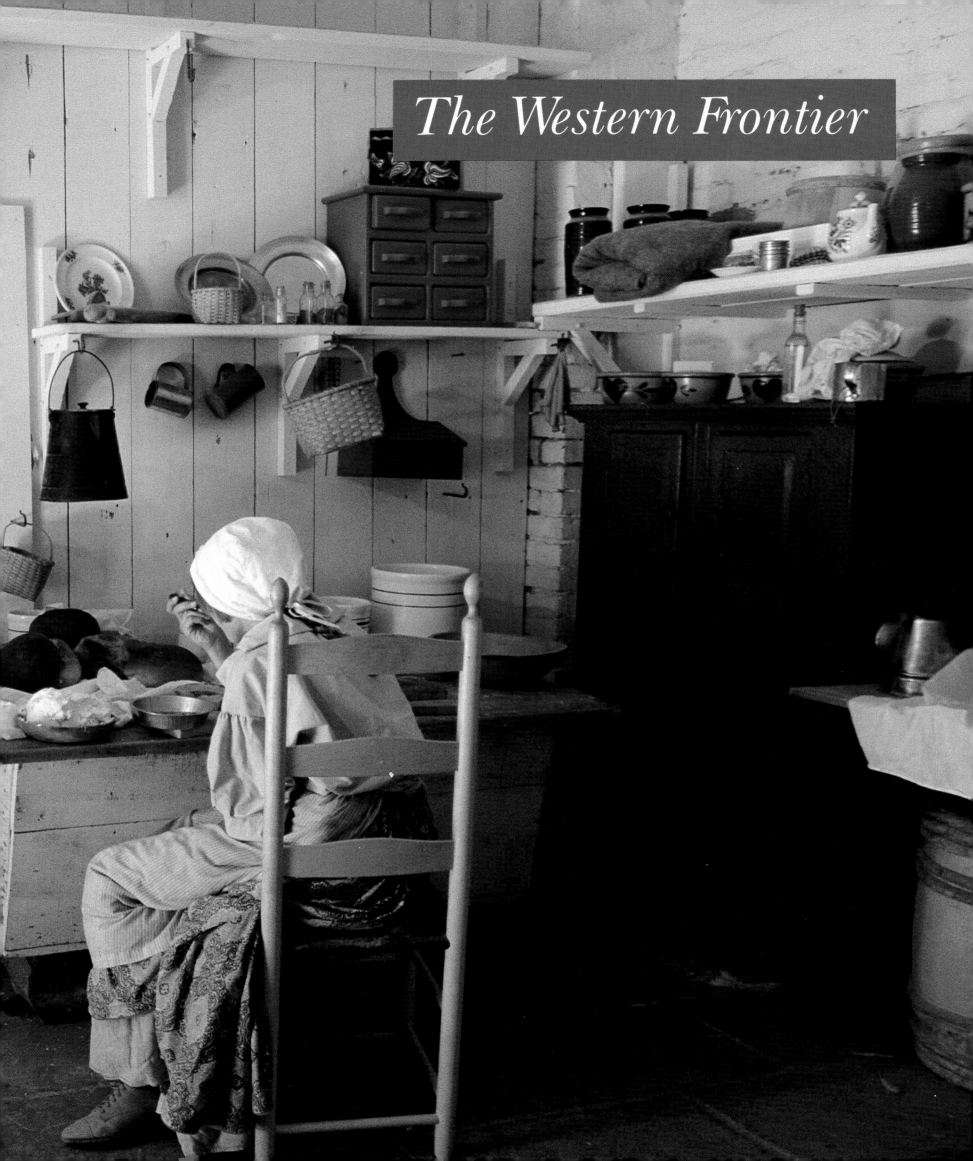

FORT UNION

NATIVE AMERICAN LIFE

Before the Europeans arrived in North America, native Americans were spread thinly across the length and breadth of the land. There were great regional and cultural differences among the tribes. In the East, for example, the Mohawk and Algonquin lived in mat-covered hogans and raised crops. The Plains Indians, among them the Cheyenne, Blackfoot, Sioux, Pawnee, and Crow, were hunters, flamboyant, mobile, and sometimes warlike. In the Southwest, the Hopi and Zuñi, descendants of the Anasazi, or ancient ones, lived in pueblos (adobe towns) on the cliffs of the Great Basin and were essentially agricultural and peaceful.

In the 16th century, the Spanish were the first Europeans to arrive in numbers. They had brought horses to America, and now hundreds of thousands of wild mustangs roamed the Plains, as did some 12 to 13 million buffalo. The horse greatly increased the mobility of the Plains Indians, whose life and rituals revolved around the buffalo hunt.

As Spanish explorers, like Francisco Vásquez de Coronado and Hernando de Soto, searched the New World for riches, they also sought to convert the Indians they met and to impose a new way of life on them. By contrast, French trappers who made their way into the continent's interior caused few changes among the tribes they encountered. In fact, they frequently adopted many aspects of native American culture.

The British settlers neither embraced Indian ways nor sought to convert tribal members to Christianity. Rather, they lived in uneasy proximity with their native American neighbors, whom they considered "barbarous heathen" (as the *Records of the Massachusetts Colony* called them). Sometimes the fragile peace between the

CHEROKEE HERITAGE CENTER

whites and the Indians exploded into violence, with raids and retaliatory forays initiated by both sides.

In the decades after the Revolutionary War, the new American nation grew dramatically through the Louisiana Purchase and the vast territories won from Mexico. These acquisitions fostered a westward migration that left the Indians fewer and fewer places to call their own. Soon, Americans believed it was their "manifest destiny" to extend their nation—and their culture—from the Atlantic to the Pacific. In pursuit of this dream, the white settlers repeatedly clashed with the Indian tribes in a series of wars that forced the Indians off their tribal lands and initiated a societal decline which has persisted into recent times. In the western Plains, the U.S. Cavalry nearly wiped out the buffalo herds as part of a strategy to force Indians onto reservations.

The last few decades have seen a considerable resurgence in Indian lore and culture. Today, wherever an Indian tribal organization is strong, there is likely to be some form of tour or lifestyle demonstration. The

Alabama and Coushatta Indians, whose woodlands reservation in East Texas was guaranteed by Sam Houston, were among the first to initiate programs for tourists. Navaho shops are plentiful along southwestern routes; guided trips into Canyon de Chelly in Arizona operate on a regular schedule.

The pueblo culture of the Southwest, past and present, has shown remarkable vitality and resilience. Tribal markings and the ruins of ancient villages are scattered like stars across the arid landscape of Arizona, New Mexico, and Utah; many have become national parks administered by the U.S. government with the advice and participation of modern tribal leaders. Their poetic and evocative names include Casa Grande, Mesa Verde, Montezuma's Castle, El Morro, Wupatki, Walnut Canyon, Tuzigoot, and Bandelier. Some others are ongoing communities which enable visitors to experience native American culture in a setting that is both traditional and contemporary. Among these towns, perhaps the most appealing is Taos, New Mexico.

(*Preceeding pages*) **The bakery at Sutter's Fort, Sacramento, California.**

Taos Pueblo

When Coronado rode across the barren lands of the Southwest in 1540, Taos Pueblo was there. It is still there, and it fascinates today's visitors as much as it did the 16th-century Spanish.

Taos, in fact, was founded 500 years before Columbus discovered the New World. The glow of the pueblo in the soft light of the setting sun caused Coronado's men to exult; at long last, they thought, they had discovered one of the legendary Indian cities of gold, perhaps El Dorado itself. Closer examination disappointed them, but they had indeed discovered one of the great cities of the time. The normally peaceful Indians, whose economy was based on agriculture, were awed by the appearance and might of the Spaniards. Coronado was an explorer, but he was soon succeeded by administrators and priests who took control of the territory from their capital in Santa Fe. In 1680, the united pueblos staged a massive revolt that drove the Spaniards back to Mexico and reestablished their own sovereignty—the only time that armed Indian resistance recovered substantial territory from Europeans. The Spanish returned in large numbers in 1693 and reasserted their rule over the pueblos of southern New Mexico, but in the north Taos held out over another five years.

Anglos came later, first as trappers and explorers and then as settlers. In 1846, as a result of the Mexican War, the region became part of the United States. An Indian uprising against the new American government in 1847 was not successful, but it took many decades to pacify the Indian tribes in the Southwest. One of the most famous frontiersmen in the region was "Kit" Carson, a fur trapper and Indian fighter who migrated from Kentucky over the Santa Fe Trail in the 1820s. During the Civil War, Carson led successful expeditions against the Mescalero Apaches, Navahos, Kiowas, and Comanches and seized their strongholds. The 1825 four-room home he purchased in 1842 in the town of Taos has been restored and furnished with Spanish colonial and territorial furniture.

The pueblo that exists today, separated into distinct north and south sections by a small river originating at the sacred Blue Lake in the nearby mountains, looks much as it did when

(*Below*) **Founded 500 years before Columbus's discovery of the New World, Taos Pueblo is a World Heritage site.**

(*Opposite*) **The shrill flute is one of the instruments used in ceremonies at Taos.**

the first Spanish explorers arrived. No matter that modern doors and windows have been added. No matter that the units are modernized inside. This is a link with ancient Indian culture unlike any other; the Taos Indians have lived in or near this pueblo for more than 1000 years.

Taos Pueblo is such an impressive example of adobe construction that it has been certified as a World Heritage site. Large multiunit mud and straw buildings, with traditional log roof braces jutting from the facades, rise abruptly from the flat, almost treeless landscape. A few rough, weathered wooden ladders, the traditional way of gaining access to upper floors, are propped against walls. The Martínez Hacienda, the oldest home in Taos, has a corner fireplace, rough wooden benches, and a hand loom.

Taos Pueblo has not only retained its identity and architectural uniqueness but, through more than 400 years of outside domination, has clung to many of its traditional ways. Bread is baked in beehive-shaped outdoor ovens. Artisans, who can be observed at work, use centuries-old techniques to create mica-flecked pottery, silver and turquoise jewelry, ceremonial drums, and buckskin clothing, all of which are sold at the pueblo. Ceremonial dances are held to mark seasonal holidays. The new year begins with a Turtle Dance, followed a few days later by the Buffalo or Deer Dance. The ritual of the Corn Dance marks the Feast of Santa Cruz in early May, the Feast of San Antonio in mid-June, the Feast of San Juan about a week later, and the Feast of Santa Ana and Santiago in late July. The two-day Feast of San Gerónimo in late September features a pole climb and foot race, a Sunset Dance, and a crafts fair.

Taos, at an elevation of 7000 feet, is the northernmost of 19 pueblos in New Mexico. Two miles north of the town of Taos, it has been preserved by the determination of the Taos–Tiwa inhabitants who live there.

(*Above*) **This elderly drummer is one of 653 people currently in residence at Taos Pueblo.**

(*Right*) **A present-day inhabitant of Taos bakes bread as her ancestors did, in beehive-shaped ovens.**

Cherokee Heritage Center

When Hernando de Soto encountered them in 1540, the Cherokees controlled some 40,000 square miles in the southern Alleghanies. In constant conflict with the early colonists, some of them fought on the side of the British in the Revolutionary War. By the early 1800s, many Cherokees had embraced the white man's ways and were living as farmers in their own self-governing nation (by treaty with the U.S. government) on about half of their original land in Georgia and Alabama. In 1838/39, the influx of white settlers led to an enforced relocation of the Cherokees, along with a number of Gulf coast tribes, to the plains of Oklahoma. Their trek westward has been called the "Trail of Tears" because at least a quarter of the 16,000 Cherokees died along the way.

In Oklahoma (then called Indian Territory) a large tract of land was reserved for each relocated tribe and for the Plains Indians who were already there. Their lives were altered in many ways. Some, like the Cherokees, built houses and again sought to follow a settled agricultural life; others, like the Plains Indians, continued a seminomadic existence. The Civil War split the tribes—even members of the same tribe—as it did the North and South. Despite promises of the U.S. government to maintain the Indian reserve, in 1889 part of the lands were opened to white settlement; the following year they were converted into the Territory of Oklahoma. In 1907, the two territories were combined and admitted into the Union as the State of Oklahoma. Today, the Indian flavor remains strong throughout the state.

One of the places preserving the Indians' rich past is the Cherokee Heritage Center (Tsa-La-Gi) at Tahlequah, Oklahoma, which includes a museum, a reconstructed village, circa 1640, an actual 1890s village, and an arboretum and herb garden. The complex occupies the site of the Cherokee Female Seminary, which opened in 1851 and burned in 1887. Three remaining columns of the seminary stand near the museum, a reminder of the emphasis that the Cherokees placed on education.

The design of the museum building, completed in 1975, is based on the Cherokee long house. Inside the 24,000-square-foot complex, a Cherokee National Hall of Fame features a reflecting pool encircled by sculptures of such celebrated tribal figures as Senator Robert L. Owen and Adm. Joseph Clark, both of whom made significant contributions to the United States.

About one-third of the museum space is devoted to archeological exhibits from ancient periods. Other major exhibits cover the rise of the Cherokee Nation; Sequoyah, who created a written Cherokee language in 1823; the removal of the Indians to Oklahoma; and the Civil War period, when Cherokee units fought on both sides.

Guided tours take visitors through two villages representing lifestyles separated by more than 300 years. In the clay-and-stick huts of the 17th-century village, living history interpreters make pottery, arrowheads, and baskets and other handicrafts in the manner of their ancestors. The 1890s Adam's Corner Rural Village, typical of the small communities in the Cherokee Nation from 1875 to 1890, has two houses furnished with replicas of simple furniture and decorations of the period (but including comforts such as a feather mattress); a schoolhouse complete with desks, blackboard, and alphabet; and a log church.

A child sleeps peacefully on deerskins at the Cherokee Heritage Center (Tsa-La-Gi) at Tahlequah, Oklahoma.

In the days before the coming of the White Man, the Cherokee used masks with exaggerated features in the dance ritual that followed the first frost.

The Murrell Home, built in 1844, is the only remnant of the type of antebellum houses built by Indians who had adopted the Anglo lifestyle. Furnished in typical period fashion, the house was owned by George Murrell, a white man who married into the prominent Cherokee family of Chief John Ross. By contrast, the Ho-Chee-Nee Chapel, a popular place for weddings, utilizes the architectural style of the ancient tribal council house. Three massive wooden poles represent the Christian Trinity, while seven beams represent the seven clans of the ancient Cherokee Nation.

Although the outdoor drama staged at the center, *The Trail of Tears*, takes its name from the enforced trek westward on which some 4000 Cherokees perished, it actually portrays a much broader sweep of tribal history.

The Cherokee Center in Tahlequah is operated by the Cherokee National Historical Society, formed in 1963. At least 50 percent of its board members belong to the tribe; the chief and deputy chief automatically are members. The ancient village opened in 1967; the drama, in 1969; and the new museum, Adam's Corner Rural Village, and Ho-Chee-Nee Chapel, in the 1970s. Prominent in the creation of the center were William Wayne Keeler, a Phillips Petroleum Company official, and M. A. Hagerstrand, a retired U.S. Army colonel.

Pockets of Cherokees and other tribes remained in the East after the trek to Oklahoma. The tribal presence is particularly strong around Cherokee, North Carolina, where a museum and open-air drama, *Unto These Hills*, explore aspects of the tribe's rich history.

(Left) **The ancient ways of the Cherokees are faithfully re-created at this 17th-century village, a major component of Tsa-La-Gi.**

(Below) **This pit at Tsa-La-Gi illustrates the importance of fire in the life of the ancient Cherokees. It was used both for cooking and making pottery.**

Fire, which the Cherokees called the "eternal flame," played a significant role in the tribal religion. They maintained blazes in front of their homes at all times.

MOUNTAIN MEN AND FUR TRADERS

The first explorers—men who followed meandering streams into the wilderness of the great western region—were fascinated by the abundance of furs which the Indians traded for brightly colored beads, blankets, and cloth. The demand for pelts in Europe was so great that soon an active frontier industry developed as a small army of trappers followed the explorers, and these, in turn, were followed by traders. The extent of their travels is truly amazing for the time: leading mules and horses, riding in Indian canoes, they crisscrossed the vastness of the Pacific Northwest.

British and American companies were active in the region early in the 19th century, following exploration by naval vessels of their nations. A New England navigator, Capt. Robert Gray, discovered the Columbia River in 1792, the same year that Capt. George Vancouver, a British explorer, charted Vancouver Island and passed through the Juan de Fuca Strait—discoveries that would later lead to disputed claims to the Pacific Northwest. But it was the expedition led by Meriwether

Lewis and William Clark from 1803 to 1806 that blazed an overland trail to the Pacific Ocean and spurred American interest in the region. Hudson's Bay Company, which dominated British trade, was already active when John Jacob Astor sent out a sea expedition in 1810 to set up a trading post at the mouth of the Columbia River, followed by an overland expedition from St. Louis, Missouri, that reached Oregon in 1812. In a few years, the annual Rendezvous, where traders, trappers, and Indians met to trade, was replaced by a string of strategically located trading posts owned by either the Hudson's Bay Company or Astor's American Fur Company. More and more settlers joined the westward movement on what came to be known as the Oregon Trail. A clash of interests among competing nations was inevitable and would ultimately lead, in 1846, to an agreement dividing the Pacific Northwest between the United States and Canada at the 49th parallel.

In addition to the trappers and traders, the rugged grandeur of the northern Rockies produced the "Mountain

FORT CLATSOP

Man," perhaps the greatest individualist in American history. He fell in love with the vastness of the wilderness and became part of it, hunting for food, and trapping furs to trade for "civilized" goods such as guns and ammunition, but mostly wanting to be left alone. For a time, the vastness of the American wilderness was his to enjoy. Soon, however, civilization would creep into the wilderness and the mountain man and trapper would pass into history.

FORT NISQUALLY

Fort Clatsop National Memorial

It rained, snowed, or hailed almost every day at Fort Clatsop during the winter of 1805/06, making life miserable for the 32 men and one woman living there. Illness was commonplace. A flea infestation and the monotony of elk meat, when it was available, did nothing for the inhabitants' dispositions. Teams of men hunted and cut wood daily, and some stood guard duty. But there were no exclamations like "Ocian in view! O! the Joy!" which their commander had written in his journal on November 7, 1805, when they first gazed on the "Great Water"—the Pacific Ocean—that so fascinated Sacagawea, the Indian woman accompanying the expedition.

That expedition was the trailblazing journey of Capt. Meriwether Lewis (President Thomas Jefferson's personal secretary) and his second in command, Capt. William Clark, both regular officers of the U.S. Army. Fort Clatsop was the outpost they had constructed near the mouth of the Columbia River in Oregon as their winter quarters. Named for the friendly Indians of the region, the site was chosen because nearby elk herds would provide a source of food, albeit a somewhat erratic one. The skins could be cured to replace the clothing and equipment tattered by the explorers in their 18-month journey through the wilderness that had begun at St. Louis, Missouri, on May 4, 1804, and proceeded up the Missouri River, over the Rocky Mountains, and down the Columbia River to the coast. Trade with the Indians, who were regarded as hard bargainers, was frequent along the way.

The military character of the log fort reflects the nature of the expedition: Captains Lewis and Clark were chosen by President Jefferson to explore the vast territory of the Louisiana Purchase, recently acquired from Napoleon's France for $15 million, map a route to the west coast, learn about the Indian

(*Opposite*) **This costumed interpreter is making a log canoe using the methods favored by Native Americans—burning and chopping—during the early years of the 19th century.**

(*Below*) **This re-creation of Fort Clatsop was constructed according to a sketch made by Cpt. William Clark, who with Cpt. Meriwether Lewis, commanded the celebrated exploratory expedition to the West Coast of North America in 1803-6.**

tribes living in the region, and (in typical Jeffersonian fashion) engage in scientific and geographic studies. The enlisted men were sturdy volunteers, all fitting Lewis's demand for "good hunters . . . capable of bearing bodily fatigue to a considerable degree." After selecting the site for their winter quarters, Lewis mapped out a strategy whose "principal object is to look out for a place to make salt, blaze the route that the men out hunting might direction to the fort, and see the probability of game in that direction."

Civilian members of the expedition included "French water men," hunters, interpreters, and Clark's black servant, York. Friendly Indians served as guides, among them Sacagawea and her fur trader husband, Toussaint Charbonneau, who joined the team in Mandan territory and stayed all the way to the Pacific and part of the way back. They took their infant son, Jean-Baptiste, with them. Clark carefully noted that, to Indians, Sacagawea's presence signified the expedition was peaceful since women were not taken along on war parties.

Fort Clatsop, functional but spare, was not intended to be permanent; the expedition gave the fort and its furnishings to the Indians when they left on March 23, 1806, to begin the long trek back to St. Louis. The Indians apparently did not make much use of it; five years after Lewis and Clark departed, it had been reduced by the wet climate to a pile of logs over-

grown by creeping vines. It was reconstructed in 1955, largely through the initiative of individuals and organizations in Oregon, to commemorate the 150th anniversary of the expedition's arrival at the Pacific. The 125-acre site was donated by the Oregon Historical Society to the federal government and became part of the National Park Service system in 1958.

The replica, which is believed to stand on the site of the original fort (although this conclusion has not thus far been confirmed by archeological excavation), is true to a sketch of the floor plan made by Clark on the elkskin cover of his journal. It consists of two parallel rows of rooms divided according to military protocol, with the officers and civilians and stores on one side and the enlisted men on the other. The rows are separated by a 20-foot-wide parade ground, closed at both ends by gates. One gate leads to a spring about 50 yards from the fort that was probably the settlement's main source of potable water, while the other leads to a landing where the expedition's boats were kept. A low watchtower protects the guard on duty during cold or inclement weather. Since no description of the fort's appearance is available beside Clark's sketch, other details are

The Indian guide Sacagawea, her husband, and their infant child lived in a small room like this at Fort Clatsop during the winter of 1805-6.

In these quarters, the leaders of the Lewis and Clark Expedition wrote voluminous notes about the Oregon territory and drew a wide range of scientific studies.

based on the writings of other first-hand sources and expert advice about the expedition and the period in which it occurred.

The captain's quarters show where the expedition's leaders labored over their extensive notes and drawings (their notes comprised more than a million words by the trip's conclusion). While at Clatsop, they reworked their journals, drew numerous maps, and organized the scientific data they had gathered. The orderly room is adjacent to the captains' quarters, and next to that is the storeroom where meat, trade items, and other goods were kept. Sacagawea, her husband, and their infant son lived in a corner room.

The enlisted men's quarters on the opposite side of the compound consist of three rooms, each housing eight or nine men and serving as an eating as well as a sleeping area. Simple log bunks with deerskins instead of slats and matresses illustrate the spartan existence of the men who lived there.

Buckskin-clad rangers carry out an active daily interpretive program from mid-June through Labor Day and on weekends in the spring. There are demonstrations on the use of muzzle-loading muskets, methods of trapping, and canoe building, as well as the making of buckskin clothing and the smoking and curing of elk meat.

The Visitors Center houses exhibits, an audio-visual introductory program, and a large statue created for the expedition's 175th anniversary, of Lewis and Clark and a Clatsop Indian, titled "Arrival," by Stanley Wanlass.

Despite its brief period of actual use, Fort Clatsop was much more than a temporary winter shelter for an exploring party. As a military post, it helped establish the American claim to the Pacific Northwest. And the expedition which it sheltered was an unqualified success. It covered more than 8000 miles by foot, horseback, keelboat, and canoe through often harsh and hostile territory and recorded a broad range of scientific and geographic data remarkable for their accuracy and detail. It not only mapped routes for later explorers and settlers to follow but awakened a young nation to the vast potential of the continent and stirred the imaginations of untold thousands who later joined the westward movement.

Fort Union

Trading posts were sometimes scenes of debauchery, as traders plied Indians and white trappers with whiskey in order to obtain their furs and buffalo hides at more attractive prices. Whole families, including children, became drunk, and violence inevitably followed. Deaths were not uncommon. Fort Union trading post at the confluence of the Missouri and Yellowstone Rivers was probably no better and no worse than others in that regard. However, a traveler recorded his impression of such events there, and thus the fort's rather shady past is documented.

Fort Union, established in 1829 by John Jacob Astor's American Fur Company, was a bustling place, with as many as 100 employees at a time. Trading went on year-round, with the Indians visiting the fort during the warm months and traders making circuits of the Indian camps during the winter. It was a cosmopolitan place for the period; one visitor observed white, black, and native Americans, as well as Englishmen, Germans, Frenchmen, Italians, Russians, and Spaniards among its inhabitants. Many of the men had wives, some being Indian women, and children were also present. A steamboat made yearly runs between the fort and St. Louis as early as the 1830s. Life was complex enough to produce a specialized division of labor: there were carpenters, masons, and blacksmiths to maintain the fort and its equipment; tinsmiths to make goods which could be traded to the Indians; and hunters to supply the post with meat. Cattle, hogs, and a vegetable garden offered other sources of nourishment. A steady stream of rough and ready adventurers passed through Fort Union, but so too did authors, scientists, and artists (including the noted painters of Indians, George Catlin and Karl Bodmer).

Naturalist James J. Audubon recorded his impressions of the outpost: "From the top of the hills we saw a grand panorama of a most extensive wilderness, with Fort Union beneath us. . . ." Because of the fort's strategic location, the federal government used it as a distribution point for annuities to Indian tribes.

Fort Union's success was due in part to its advantageous location and in part to the quality of its management. It was fortunate to have a succession of good managers, or *bourgeois*, starting with Kenneth McKenzie, who supervised construction of the post. An ambitious Scotsman who had learned the fur trade in Canada, McKenzie made Fort Union the principal trading post on the upper Missouri. The fort also benefited from the relative quiescence of the Indians within its domain. By 1847, however, the more aggressive Sioux began migrating to the area under the pressure of white settlement farther downstream, and the fort's luck began to change. When, at the same time, the European market for beaver pelts collapsed, the fort fell into a period of decline. In 1867, it was closed and dismantled to provide building materials for Fort Buford, an Army post some 2 miles away.

The resurrection of Fort Union began in 1966 when the National Park Service acquired the site. At that time, only ridges and mounds of earth identified the stone foundations of the

A sharpshooting "trapper" draws a bead in a marksmanship demonstration at Fort Union. A keen eye was essential for those who lived off of what they could kill in the wilderness.

(*Above*) **A buffalo hide, drying in the sun at Fort Union, demonstrates the method used to cure hides.**

(*Right*) **A smartly dressed member of the fort's interpretive staff welcomes visitors to Bourgeois House.**

post's palisades and bastions. Excavations between 1968 and 1972 uncovered the foundations of these structures and the location of the main house and other buildings, walkways, and fence lines. Artifacts were unearthed that indicated trading methods and a relatively comfortable lifestyle, one that even included the latest fashions of the day. Among the relics that were discovered and are now on display are pottery and china, cooking and eating utensils, mirrors, bracelets, and metal parts of firearms.

A program to partially restore the fort to its 1851 appearance was started in 1979, based on sketches by Swiss artist Rudolph Kurz and later illustrations and photographs made in 1866. The 63-foot-high flagpole was completed in June 1985. Two years later saw the dedication of the imposing Bourgeois House. The white two-story structure boasts two wings, porches with black-painted posts, and a red roof and chimney. The interior is a representation since its exact appearance is not known, but two sets of original hearthstones are incorporated into the structure. The Bourgeois House now serves as the Visitors Center and displays a variety of historical exhibits.

The ruins of Fort Buford, a state historic site, complement the presentation at Fort Union.

Starting a fire with dried grass and buffalo chips was a fundamental and essential wilderness skill.

Fort Nisqually

Even in the wilderness of the Northwest, officials of the Hudson's Bay Company of London and its subsidiary, the Puget Sound Agricultural Company, kept good records. They made daily, handwritten entries about the construction of outposts, the utilization of manpower, significant arrivals and departures, and sometimes even anecdotes and the weather. These records served as an important resource in the re-creation of Fort Nisqually, one of the fortified camps established by the company as part of its fur trading activities in the northwestern United States and Canada.

Fort Nisqually began as a single house, raised in 1832 on the shores of Puget Sound by the company's chief trader, Archibald MacDonald. The following year, he supervised the construction of a more elaborate post—primarily for fur trading—about half a mile away from the house. Indians and traders brought large numbers of beaver pelts to Fort Nisqually, whose name derived from an Indian word for the waving prairie grass of the region. Indians especially prized the blankets offered in trade at the fort. Indeed, these blankets became such symbols of prestige that each could command two pelts in a trade.

By 1840, the overkilling of animals and the waning popularity of beaver felt hats in Europe caused a dramatic decline in the fur trade. But Fort Nisqually did not fall to ruin, as did other outposts. Rather, it fell back on what had already become an expanding secondary business. The rich soil helped make the fort the main station of the Puget Sound Agricultural Company, a subsidiary designed to supply grain and produce, as well as salted salmon and beef, to the Hudson's Bay Company's various posts and markets. Longhorns from Mexican California thrived on the tall grass around Nisqually. Sheep herds were also started.

In 1843, a successor fort of the same name was constructed on a site near Sequalitchew Creek that provided more land for grazing and farming. Soon, American settlers began arriving in Oregon in increasing numbers. The territory was claimed by Great Britain, but that did not stop the pioneers. When British warships entered Nisqually Bay to protect Hudson's Bay Company property, it seemed for a time that the United States and Britain might go to war over the region. In the boundary dispute that erupted, Americans wanted the border in the Northwest placed at latitude 54°40′N, the southern boundary of Russian Alaska, and "Fifty-Four Forty or Fight" became the Democrats' campaign slogan in the presidential election of 1844, which James K. Polk won. Ultimately, however, the Canadian boundary was extended to the coast at latitude 49°N in the Treaty of 1846. And, in the end, the Hudson's Bay Company abandoned the Nisqually site and received compensation for it from the U.S. government.

The original site of Fort Nisqually near Du Pont, Washington, was acquired in 1906 by the Du Pont Powder Company. By then, only the Factor's House and a chicken coop from the second site remained. These were relocated to Point Defiance Park in Tacoma and restored during the 1930s by the Young Men's Business Club and Chamber of Commerce. The effort to reconstruct the fort as it looked in its heyday (from 1843 to 1859) has been ongoing.

This bastion, one of two built at Fort Nisqually in 1848, is armed with a cannon. The ground floor served as the fort's jail.

(*Above*) **The interior of the Tyee House re-creates the spartan lifestyle that Fort Nisqually's first managers endured in the 1840s. The house also served as an office.**

(*Opposite*) **A costumed interpreter representing an early Scottish inhabitant of Fort Nisqually selects an axe from among the implements leaning against the wall of the New Grannary.**

Costumed interpreters portray the people who frequented the log-walled fort—sailors from ships that harbored nearby, company employees, trappers, and Indians. A Queen Victoria Birthday Celebration in May reminds visitors of the fort's British ancestry, and a brigade encampment in mid-August recalls the martial aspects of the commercial frontier outpost.

The restored frame Factor's House was the residence of the senior official at the fort. It was quite comfortable by frontier standards, with an imposing parlor, a dining hall, and two bedrooms on the ground floor, each with a fireplace and wallpaper coverings. About 30 percent of the original 1854 building, including doors and windows, are incorporated in the restoration, which now houses a small museum of fur trade relics, a shop, and offices.

The New Granary, the complex's other original building, was the second structure constructed to house the bounty of the nearby fields. Listed in the National Register of Historic Places, the squared timber building is typical of Hudson's Bay Company architecture and one of the few remaining examples of Canadian-style construction of the period in North America. About 60 percent of the original wood was salvaged in the restoration. Currently, it is furnished as a typical warehouse of the era.

The reconstructed 20-foot-high log stockade, enclosing a large quadrangle, resembles the original which was completed in 1849. It had two gates: a small "water gate" that provided access to a nearby stream, and the main gate (called the orchard gate), through which wagons could be driven. A storm knocked down part of one wall in 1855; the rest, too deteriorated to be salvaged, was torn down in 1858. The bastions—a square one at the northwest corner whose ground floor typically served as a jail, and a six-sided one at the southeast corner—are armed with cannon just as the originals were.

Other reconstructed buildings include the Tyee House, one of the first to be built at the fort and the home of the manager until the Factor's House was built; the one-room blockhouse, the principal sanctuary in the event of attack before the stockade was constructed; and the Men's Dwelling, built in 1846 for laborers at Nisqually. In all, 15 structures are enclosed within the walls of the fort.

Bent's Old Fort

No site in the history of western trade was better positioned to exploit developing trends than Bent's Old Fort near La Junta. It was one of the earliest outposts deep in the heart of Indian country, and it was situated at a crossroads of the major overland trails. Thus, it was a magnet for Indians, trappers, mountain men, American and Mexican traders, adventurers, and settlers. In time, it became a principal staging area for military action in New Mexico as well.

Bent's Old Fort, now a national historic site, was constructed in 1833 at a time when Mexico disputed U.S. claims to Colorado. The dispute continued until the Mexican War, after which Mexico relinquished all claims to the Southwest. William Bent, the fort's founder, was one of the first traders to venture into this wilderness of valleys and mountains, where he traded with the Mexicans and Indians, sometimes in partnership with his brother Charles and Ceran St. Vrain, and sometimes independently. Although officially called Fort William, it was commonly known as Bent's Fort.

Nothing William Bent had done previously compared to what he would accomplish after he built the large adobe trading post on the Arkansas River. An early advocate of fair trade with the Indians, Bent discouraged the use of whiskey. His marriage to the daughter of a southern Cheyenne leader and his work to achieve peace between the tribes gave the fort its special status as a neutral ground were intertribal councils and parleys between Indian chiefs and U.S. government officials could be held. In 1846, it was designated as the Indian Agency headquarters for the region. It was also the headquarters of Bent, St. Vrain & Company, formed by the partners to engage in trade with Santa Fe.

The success of the trading post ultimately became one of the elements of its undoing. The Mexican War made it strategically important as a supply point for the dragoons and Missouri Volunteers under Gen. Stephen W. Kearny who were engaged in the conquest of New Mexico. Indians who had previously come there to trade avoided the fort because of the presence of a large number of whites. The fort's role as a storehouse for military supplies and its large military population interfered with other trade as well. Moreover, the army horses, as well as those of settlers and gold prospectors en route to New Mexico, overgrazed the surrounding countryside and otherwise unbalanced the ecology. The fort's demise was hastened when Charles Bent, appointed the first governor of New Mexico Territory, was assassinated by Taos Indians; and then a cholera epidemic (apparently transmitted by a passing wagon train) decimated the nearby Indian population.

The "trader" at Bent's Old Fort totes his accounts during a respite between bargaining sessions with Indians and trappers. Behind him are some of the goods he will offer in trade for furs.

In its heyday, the parade ground of Bent's Old Fort was crowded
with armed trappers like this fellow.

In 1849, William Bent vacated the Old Fort—he may have used explosives and a torch to partially destroy it—and built Bent's New Fort, nearly 40 miles down the Arkansas River near Lamar. The new trading post was never successful, however, and in 1860 he sold it to the army, which used it as a fortified commissary. Today, only earthworks and a marker identify the second outpost.

However, the site of Bent's Old Fort was protected by the Daughters of the American Revolution, which sold it to the State Historical Society of Colorado in the early 1950s. The Natonal Park Service acquired the site in 1963. Additional land, acquired in 1978, brought the national park to a total of about 850 acres.

The old adobe fort has been reconstructed just as it was. Begun in 1976, the reconstruction took about a year to complete; it was based largely on archeological digs made by Trinidad State Junior College, as well as historical accounts and excavations undertaken by the National Park Service in the 1960s. The quadrangular outpost has 15-foot-high, 2-foot-thick adobe walls with musket loopholes and two large round corner bastions, where cannon were mounted in the 1840s. Rooms are built along the interior wall of the fort to create a single structure. An adobe powder magazine and a well are in the large courtyard.

All of the elements of the fort are open to public view and provide a vivid portrait of life in a frontier fort of the period. The 30 rooms in the walls and towers are furnished as they would have been in 1846 when Bent presided over his empire. Among them are the living quarters, kitchen, and dining room, whose rough furniture illustrates how crude life was on the frontier. There are also three warehouses, an Indian trade room, a carpenter shop, and even a billiard room.

(*Above*) **The barracks room at Bent's Old Fort was known as the dragoon infirmary as the 1833 structure was used to house sick and injured soldiers who were passing through the region. Laborers also lived there.**

(*Left*) **The adobe walls of Bent's Old Fort were a welcome sight to settlers trying to reach Oregon in covered wagons like the one shown here. It was also a gathering place for Indians and trappers seeking to sell pelts for finished goods.**

FROM LOG CABINS TO BOOM TOWNS

The advance of civilization was incremental. In the years before the Civil War, wagon trains carried an ever-increasing number of settlers to the west coast. After the U.S.–Canadian boundary in the Northwest was set at the 49th parallel, that part belonging to the United States became the Oregon Territory in 1848; the formerly disputed area between the Columbia River and the new border was split off as the Territory of Washington in 1853. Meanwhile, California and the New Mexico Territory were ceded to the United States as a result of the Treaty of 1848 ending the Mexican War. The United States paid Mexico $15 million and assumed the latter's obligations to Americans, up to $3.25 million. In so doing, the United States gained some 500,000 square miles of new land.

On the eve of the peace settlement, a major discovery was made at Sutter's Mill on the American River in northern California. The sudden influx of the "forty-niners"—prospectors, for-

THE STUHR MUSEUM OF THE PRAIRIE PIONEER

tune seekers, and sundry ne'er-do-wells—brought great excitement and sudden wealth to a region that previously had been peacefully rural. Silver strikes later would have the same effect on states like Colorado and Nevada. Most of the gold towns went through stages. They began as violent tent encampments which were, in turn, succeeded by lusty towns, where prices skyrocketed and fortunes were made and lost. Some towns died after the mines played out and the fortune seekers moved on to new strikes, but other communities survived and became stable places with law, order, and other trappings of civilization.

Not all frontier towns arose from the quest for gold and silver, of course. The coming of the railroad gave rise to rip-roaring communities that were the termini for long cattle drives from Texas. Uninhibited cowboys, coming off a trail drive that lasted several months, came to town to drink and fight and exchange in gunplay, eventually forcing the locals to hire tough, straight-shooting lawmen who were often closer in spirit to the men they were hired to control than to the average peaceable citizen.

The quest for religious freedom also gave rise to new communities, notably those in Utah which were settled by Mormons seeking freedom from religious persecution back east.

With the completion of the transcontinental railroad in May 1869 and the settlement of inland farming and grazing areas, the wilderness was gradually being tamed. And by 1890, according to the U.S. Census, the frontier was closed. For better or worse, "civilization" was asserting itself.

LAND OFFICE, OLD COWTOWN MUSEUM

ROSE TREE INN, TOMBSTONE, ARIZONA

Sutter's Fort

Before gold was discovered, California was not getting the attention it deserved. After the discovery, it received more than it could handle. Indeed, it was inundated by the "gold rush," a surge of frantic people all hellbent on finding the yellow metal. Distance was no obstacle. People spent months traveling overland or by ship around Cape Horn to reach San Francisco, the closest port to the goldfields. Many of the great clippers ended their careers in San Francisco Bay, abandoned when crews ran off in search of gold.

The man responsible for this hysteria was an unlikely catalyst, John Augustus Sutter, a Swiss immigrant who had failed in a number of business ventures in Europe and the United States and had wandered to both Alaska and Hawaii in search of his niche in life. He arrived in California in 1839 and led a small party of colonists up the Sacramento and American Rivers. They landed at what would become 28th street in the future city of Sacramento. Becoming a Mexican citizen in order to obtain a land grant of nearly 48,000 acres, he named his colony New Helvetia after his homeland of Switzerland. The fort that he built in 1840 was intended to provide a secure focal point for a colony devoted largely to agriculture and the

distillation of spirits. Within a few years, New Helvetia had 4000 cattle, 3000 sheep, and 1700 horses and mules.

Sutter adopted an open, helpful attitude toward newcomers. He recruited settlers from Switzerland and Germany, as well as the United States, and gave them free shelter and supplies upon arrival. The fort, which could accommodate as many as 300 people, was always available as a temporary refuge. Sutter tried to maintain good relations with all parties when U.S. Army and Navy detachments occupied California in 1846 during the Mexican War and when the Bear Flag Republic was ceded to the United States by the peace treaty of 1848. (It joined the Union as a free state in 1850.)

The discovery of gold 40 miles from the fort by one of Sutter's employees, James Marshall, changed the life of New Helvetia forever. Workmen simply walked away from the mill, whose grindstones eventually were stolen or sold, and its tannery, where hides were left to rot. Squatters took control of much of the land, and the fort became a way station for pros-

Pioneer women became adept at open-air cooking. That method of preparing food, demonstrated at Sutter's Fort, sustained them on the long trek west.

(*Above*) **This musician coaxes a lively tune out of his accordion while several of his companions listen. Singing and dancing offered settlers rare moments of relaxation on the frontier.**

(*Opposite*) **The main gate of Sutter's Fort was large enough to admit wagons but could be closed against attack.**

pectors and miners. Sutter was ruined. He sold the fort in 1849 in order to satisfy some of his creditors. Eventually he moved to Lititz, Pennsylvania, where he pressed Congress to compensate him for his colonization work and loss of property. He died in 1880 without receiving it.

After Sutter's departure, the adobe fort deteriorated quickly. Within a decade, little remained except the Central Building, which was acquired in 1890 by the Native Sons of the Golden West in one of the earliest historical conservation efforts. The organization deeded the property to the state in 1891, which began soon afterward to reconstruct the fort based on an 1848 map that appeared in a German emigration booklet.

Now a state historic park surrounded by the hustle and bustle of the state capital, the reconstructed Sutter's Fort is rectangular, with walls 15 feet high and 2½ feet thick. Bastions armed with cannon are located at the northwest and southeast corners. The flat 320-foot-long courtyard is broken by the restored Central Building, a well, a saw pit, a few trees, and a

flagpole which normally flies the American flag but also flies the standard of Mexico on appropriate ceremonial occasions. Most of the living quarters and work areas line the interior wall of the fort, with two open stables along the north wall.

Interior rooms in the wall are furnished to reflect many of the significant daily activities during Sutter's time, including baking and cooking, leatherworking, and the making of wine and brandy. Some chambers are used as storerooms to reflect their original function, while others are preserved as living quarters since a cadre of transient and permanent residents made the fort their home in Sutter's day. There are also guardrooms flanking the large main gate on the south side of the fort. These were used by Sutter's defense force, comprised largely of blacks and Indians.

Static displays with push-button commentaries provide insight into the kind of life that existed in the fort in the 1840s, as do various demonstrations. An effort is also made to illustrate the difference between the life in the interior of California and that in more developed coastal cities.

The two-story Central Building (plus basement) houses Sutter's office and residence, with its comfortable dining room and living quarters. A clerk's office and doctor's office occupy ground floor rooms, and there is a wine cellar and an armory in the basement.

In a guardroom, one of Sutter's "watchmen" carefully prepares loads for his weapon, using bulk powder.

Visitors should bear in mind that many of New Helvetia's activities occurred outside the fort. Some of Sutter's guests and vaqueros were housed in other dwellings, and the tannery was situated on the American River. Marshall was supervising construction of a sawmill on the river's South Fork when he discovered gold.

The largest collection of buildings from the gold rush period is located in Old Sacramento, the historic quarter of the city that once served as the transportation and supply center for mines in the Mother Lode country. Sacramento was also for a time the western terminus of the transcontinental communica-

tions network, including the Pony Express and overland stage companies. It became the state capital in 1854. Forty-four historic structures that once housed banks, express offices, and 180 other businesses and services survive in Old Sacramento. Their exteriors are preserved, and the interiors have been converted to modern uses such as shops and restaurants.

The site of Marshall's precedent-shattering discovery is preserved at the Marshall Gold Discovery State Historic Park at Coloma, California, where the setting is re-created showing what life was like in the gold camps.

Old Cowtown Museum

A poster at the Old Cowtown Museum in Wichita sings the praises of "Warner's Sure Cure." Perhaps patent medicines like this provided some of the energy needed to settle the vast and often inhospitable land of the American West. Wichita was as energetic as any town on the frontier. It was also one of the most successful. Citizens were so eager to have the railroad come there that they formed their own company and sold bonds to finance it. The first sod houses quickly became frame and brick structures as cattlemen drove their herds toward the railroad along the Chisholm Trail.

Old Cowtown, a re-created village incorporating a few vintage structures, reflects Wichita's pioneering period from 1865 to 1880, with 63 buildings on a 17-acre site. Four residences, two churches, a hotel, a carpenter's shop, and other commercial enterprises are stocked with more than 12,000 artifacts and other objects.

Several residences are open to guided tours. The Darius Sales Munger House, built in 1868/69 by a town founder and partner in the Wichita Land and Town Company, is the town's oldest surviving house and is listed on the National Register of Historic Places. Considered the most substantial building in the community, the residence at times doubled as a post office, a church, and a public gathering place. Perhaps the most unusual residence in the complex is the "Horse Thief" Cabin, an origi-

(*Above*) **The prominent place of the harness and saddle shop at the Old Cowtown Museum indicates its importance to Wichita, which was a wagon freighting center.**

(**Left**) **"Gambler" Charley Whitworth savors a "seegar," a symbol of manliness in cowtowns like Wichita.**

nal house built about 1868, which more than likely served as the temporary home of an early settler. Its location beside the Chisholm Trail may have recommended it to men who raided passing herds.

In their early stages, frontier towns usually had a closely packed business area of frame structures. Fire was such a hazard that creation of a volunteer fire company was a priority item. A major part of Wichita burned in 1875. The Frontier Fire Company that fought the blaze was formed in 1872 by Wichita businessmen. It is recalled at the firehouse strategically located at the head of the main business street near the general store, where the gunsmith was also located. Other businesses included the J. P. Allen Drug Store, the first such enterprise in the town, and M. M. Fechheimer Clothing Store, which sold not only finished garments but fabrics, including cloth for women's

(*Above*) **Canned food, thread, and a spare lamp, plus a posted inventory, suggest that the pantry of the 1874 Murdock House was well stocked and carefully organized.**

dresses. The *Eagle* building, restored in 1988, re-creates a working 1870s newspaper plant, ready for the printer to set the type and go to press. And, like any good cowtown, Wichita had accommodations for transients. The rooms of the Southern Hotel are well suited to meet the needs of cattlemen, salesmen, and gamblers passing through town.

Old Cowtown is an active place. A 47-member Re-enactment Society and the 20-woman Dixie Lee Saloon Girls help bring life to the wooden sidewalks, unpaved streets, and authentic buildings. Theme weekends cover such subjects as a land auction and frontier funeral. Politicians talk at an old-time rally, and a young couple "ties the knot." Entre Nous Club members perform polkas, schottiches, and other period dances on special occasions. "Sheriff" Henry Dunning straps on his pistol to take a turn around the town. Youngsters roll their hoops and stare with wonderment at the cowboys in string ties and Stetsons. Dance hall girls flash their petticoats to the music in Fritz Snitzler's Saloon, one of 15 that did a booming business in Wichita in 1873.

Programs marking holidays include an 1870s-style Fourth of July celebration and a Christmas-Through-the-Windows program, when the historic buildings are adorned with wreaths and other greenery, and handmade decorations.

Old Cowtown Museum began as an effort to save an old boarding house and the 1870 First Presbyterian Church and parsonage. The museum opened in 1950 and has expanded bit by bit over the years through joint private–governmental cooperation. More than 15 new exhibits or renovations have occurred since 1987. A three-phase plan for future development includes an 1870s working farm.

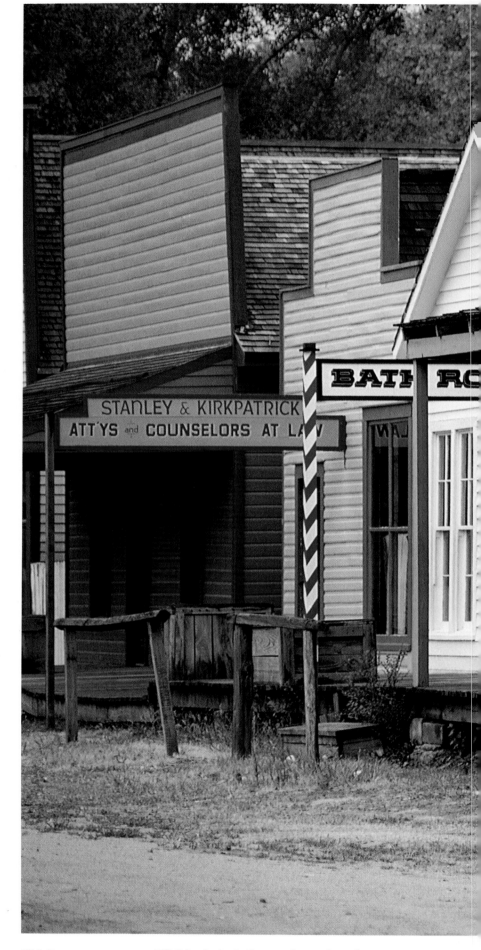

Old Cowtown recreates Wichita in its infancy when a board sidewalk lined the town's main street and a drug store, post office, barber shop, and attorney's office were among the principal commercial enterprises.

Historic Tombstone

Boot Hill headstones for the Clantons and Tom McLaury suggest that their shootout with the Earps and 'Doc' Holliday was something other than the fair fight painted in legend.

They call it the town "too tough to die," but Tombstone was saved from extinction only through the efforts of an enterprising group of 20th-century merchants and residents who were eager to preserve their heritage. Today, the town is a thriving community whose main business is tourism. It may impress some visitors as too commercial, but the former near-ghost town is almost as prosperous now as it was when silver was king.

If most people in southeastern Arizona in the 1870s had had their way, Tombstone would have been a ranching center. The area around the town was well suited for grazing, and consequently a number of ranches were started there. But marauding Apaches had scared off most of the early ranchers by the time Ed Schieffelin and his partners found the vein that ultimately would prove to be the richest in the area, producing large quantities of silver and gold. Some of the most famous mines in the Old West—Toughnut, Lucky Cuss, Contention, Emerald, and Good Enough among them—were in the Tombstone area. Some even extended under the town.

Schieffelin was a typical prospector—incorrigible. He had looked for precious metal all over the West, taking a steady job only when he needed a grubstake for his next stab at the mother lode. But even Schieffelin could not dream that the ore samples he collected in southeastern Arizona would assay at $2000 a ton! Within a few years of Shieffelin's discovery, a dozen major mines were producing a steady steam of ore. Shieffelin called the town that sprang up Tombstone because that's what he was told he would find by prospecting in the region—his tombstone. Development was as perverse as it was rapid; although the city plan had envisioned Frémont Street as the hub, Allen Street became the center of business activity. Two-thirds of the buildings held saloons or gambling halls catering to the desires of prospectors, miners, cowboys, and those who hoped to benefit from their labors. At night, the town came alive, and the evening air was filled with the sound of raucous laughter, brash music, heated arguments, and occasional gunfire.

Despite the rowdy start, the town grew rapidly. By 1891, it had 10,000 inhabitants, a large percentage of whom were gamblers, gunslingers, prostitutes, and miners who would move on when and if the mines played out. Gunfights and lynchings were so common that a large cemetery had to be set aside. Some of the most legendary characters in the West earned their reputations in Tombstone. Indeed, the shootout at the town's O.K. Corral, in which the Earp brothers and "Doc" Holliday defeated the Clantons and McLaurys, has entered the national folklore as the classic example of a gunfight. But Tombstone's heyday was brief. The town wilted when water began filling the mine shafts and the cost of pumping it out became prohibitive.

Tombstone's historic area, bounded roughly by Frémont, Toughnut, and 6th Streets and U.S. 50, depicts the community at its peak in the 1880s. Some of the buildings antedate an 1882 fire, whereas others were constructed afterward. Attractions such as the Crystal Palace, Bird Cage Theatre, and O.K. Corral make Allen Street the main drag today, just as it was in the city's golden days.

At the O.K. Corral, visitors pass through a stagecoach office to enter a re-creation of the famous gunfight. Life-size manne-

**Dressed in black, the "Earp brothers" and "'Doc' Holliday" leave
for their rendezvous with the Clanton gang at the O.K. Corral.**

Allen Street was the center of business activity in the town "too tough to die." Some of the saloons that lined this street stayed open 24 hours a day in Tombstone's heyday.

quins show the positions of the Earp brothers and "Doc" Holliday at the start of the fight, along with the positions of their opponents, Ike and Bill Clanton, Frank and Tom McLaury, and Billy Claiborne. Adjacent to the corral are the stable, as well as a building housing photographs of Tombstone during the Earp era and the period when Apache chief Geronimo led raids in the area.

Elsewhere are the 1882 brick jail, whose first floor was occupied by a fire company, and the Wells Fargo Museum and General Store, which displays 75,000 Old West artifacts including silver bullion.

The Crystal Palace, the most famous of the town's saloons, has been restored inside and out to its appearance in 1879, the year it was built. A long bar, which in the 1880s stayed open all night and accommodated even Marshal Wyatt Earp on occasion, extends almost the depth of the building.

The 1881 Bird Cage Theatre, which operated nonstop for nine years, was once described as the "wildest, wickedest night spot between Basin Street and the Barbary Coast." The rough audiences preferred cancan dancers and bawdy shows, but accepted touring vaudeville performers as well. The name of the theater derives from cages, occupied by prostitutes, which hung from the ceiling. Declared a Historic Landmark of the Amer-

ican West in 1934, the theater is preserved in its original state, largely because it was sealed after the mines were closed. The handsome cherry-wood bar with a large mirror and the famous painting of Fatima, punctured by six bullet holes, are located just where they were in 1881. The stage, chandeliers, and curtains in the main hall are also original.

Those wishing to experience the life of a miner vicariously can take a tour through the Good Enough Mine—one of the claims staked by Shieffelin—which runs under the town. The mine was a productive source of silver in the 1880s.

Despite its hell-raising reputation, Tombstone had a gentler side which can be seen at Schieffelin Hall, where the "good" people of the community gathered for entertainment. The large adobe structure has been carefully restored to its original appearance. St. Paul's Episcopal Church, built in 1882 and the oldest Protestant church still standing in Arizona, was among the institutions exerting a religious influence.

The brick Tombstone Courthouse, built in 1882, was the scene of many a court battle over mine ownership. Now a state park, it houses a historical museum featuring Wyatt Earp memorabilia and local historical items. A reconstructed gallows in the yard shows how justice was often summarily dispensed.

From the gallows, the departed would have moved to the rocky cemetery on the outskirts of town. There, one finds inscriptions as colorful as the men and women whose graves they mark. George Johnson, it seems, was "Hanged by Mistake," while an unidentified teamster was "Killed by Indians."

This adobe wall on Allen Street gives entrance to the O.K. Corral, site of the most famous gunfight in the Old West.

Historic Deadwood

A poker hand of aces and eights is still regarded in some quarters as the "dead man's hand." That was what U.S. Marshal James Butler ("Wild Bill") Hickok was holding on August 2, 1876, when Jack McCall shot him in the back of the head in Deadwood's Saloon No. 10. Numerous other stories from this notorious gold town have entered the national folklore thanks to Calamity Jane and other oldtimers. Calamity, who outlived Bill by 30 years, claimed to be secretly married to him, although he already had a wife elsewhere. At any rate, she is buried beside him in Deadwood's Mount Moriah Cemetery, as she wanted to be.

Deadwood—the most famous of the gold towns in the Black Hills—was the kind of place that produced legends. It was known far and wide for its unhibited hell-raising, risk-all, do-all breed of men. It was also known for its gambling halls; so much so that card sharps assembled there from all over the West. Reputation aside, however, Deadwood was really no worse than any other gold-mining town; they were all wide open at the beginning.

The strike that created Deadwood did not exactly come as a surprise. The Black Hills of South Dakota had long been known to contain gold, but the rugged forested wilderness was sacred to the Sioux Indians and had been reserved to them by treaty. In 1874, Lt. Col. George Armstrong Custer, following in the wake of a few daring prospectors who had already entered the region (and not all of whom had returned), led an exploratory expedition to confirm the existence of gold in the Black Hills. Once the strike was ascertained, the treaty with the Sioux certainly could not withstand the pressures of the gold seekers. The U.S. government therefore began negotiating with the Sioux again. In the autumn of 1875, prospectors were busily searching for the big strike, and by the next spring some 25,000 hopefuls had poured into Deadwood, making it a boom town.

Today, Deadwood is a small 20th-century town. But for the benefit of history and the tourists who come to visit, its Wild West past lives on. For example, the murder of "Wild Bill," who normally sat with his back to a wall to prevent such an eventuality, is recalled daily during the summer months at the reenactment of McCall's trial. McCall was acquitted by a local jury, then rearrested and retried by another, and finally hanged in Yankton. The Deadwood Central Railroad, pulled by an old steam engine, maneuvers past abandoned mine shafts and a waterfall. A covered wagon is "attacked" by Indians. A conducted tour of a 100-year-old tunnel constructed by Chinese laborers features a simulated opium den, as well as Chinese religious carvings and other artifacts. Although the Chinese were often blamed during the period for the opium trade, others trafficked in drugs as well.

The annual "Days of '76" celebration recalls Deadwood's heyday with particular fervor, and the usual history program is supplemented with a rodeo and parade.

Although an 1879 fire destroyed much of the city, Main Street has been restored to its 1876 appearanced. It is a registered National Historic Landmark with the "feel" of a gold boom town. Keno and craps tables and antique slot machines in the Old Days of Deadwood Museum recall that favorite pastime of the gold-mining town, gambling. More than 70 villains, Indians, pioneers, and other Wild West characters fill the Ghosts

The "king of pistoleers," James Butler "Wild Bill" Hickok, was shot while playing poker and is buried in Deadwood's Mt. Moriah Cemetery. "Calamity" Jane Canary rests nearby.

Piano music fills Saloon No. 10, as it did when the bar was "Wild Bill" Hickok's favorite gambling place.

This trophy wall in Saloon No. 10 recalls some of the famous citizens, desperadoes, and incidents in Deadwood's colorful history.

The ornate spire of the Deadwood Courthouse symbolizes the moment when each miner, gambler, and gunfighter ceased to be a law unto himself and law and order began.

of Deadwood Gulch—Western Heritage Wax Museum, not far from a Korczak Ziolkowski statue of "Wild Bill" Hickok. A mile west of town is the Broken Boot Gold Mine, which operated from 1878 to 1904. Conducted tours of the sometimes wet shaft show visitors what a gold miner's life was like during the period.

A number of other attractions in the Black Hills complement the Deadwood story. Perhaps the most intriguing of these is the Homestake Gold Mine at Lead, South Dakota, the most productive gold mine in the Western Hemisphere, having yielded more than $1 billion in gold since its first lode was discovered in 1876. Bear Butte, a sacred mountain to the Sioux, stands as it did in the 19th century when it served as a landmark guiding prospectors into the hills. Custer State Park preserves the kind of wilderness into which they ventured in 1876 and has a sizable herd of buffalo.

Ziolkowski, the artist who sculpted Deadwood's Hickok statue, began work in 1939 on a monumental 563-foot-high statue of the great Sioux warrior Crazy Horse, to be carved out of Thunderhead Mountain, as the Indian equivalent of Mount Rushmore. Visitors may view a 16-foot-high scale model of the work and can observe progress from a distance.

Stuhr Museum of the Prairie Pioneer

GRAND ISLAND, NEBRASKA

The first houses built by settlers on the prairie were made of sod, the most readily available building material. Such dwellings were damp and often uncomfortable, but they saw many a farm family through the cold, snowy winters and the hot summers. Life on the Great Plains was generally hard and usually lonely—so hard that many gave up and moved on—but the fertile land soon enabled those who persevered to improve their homes, add barns, and acquire wagons to increase their social mobility. Market towns developed in strategic locations to supply their needs and export their products. Between 1860 and 1890, the most important "town builder" was the railroad.

Stuhr Museum of the Prairie Pioneer relates the story of the prairie town builders in a 200-acre living history museum near Grand Island, Nebraska. Most of the complex's 60 structures have been moved to the site and restored to their original function and appearance. Two exhibit buildings are open year-round, while re-creations can be visited during the warm months.

A portion of the museum known as the Railroad Town—an ideal site for making movies of the taming of the West—re-creates the kind of railroad hub that transformed the prairie lifestyle in the latter half of the 19th century.

Horse-drawn buggies move slowly along the streets past the town store, the *Platte River Independent* office, and other buildings. They also pass Elftman's Barber Shop, where the men gather to discuss business, politics, crops, and the weather, and the 1888 Danish Lutheran Church with its skirted steeple and old country facade. It and the school are all that is left of the community of Runelsburg, whose founder mistakenly thought the railroad would pass through *his* town. The old Ovina post office and store which once served a sheep ranch community are located on a spur.

During the summer months, costumed interpreters give life to the village. The town marshal patrols the streets. "Aunt Hattie" gossips with neighbors. A suffragette eagerly tries to bend the ear of anyone who will listen. A telegrapher hunches over his key in his office at the depot, while a short distance away the blacksmith works in his shop.

Pianos and pot-bellied stoves like these in the music room and parlor of the Millisen House at the Stuhr Museum were prominent features of many Western homes late in the 19th century.

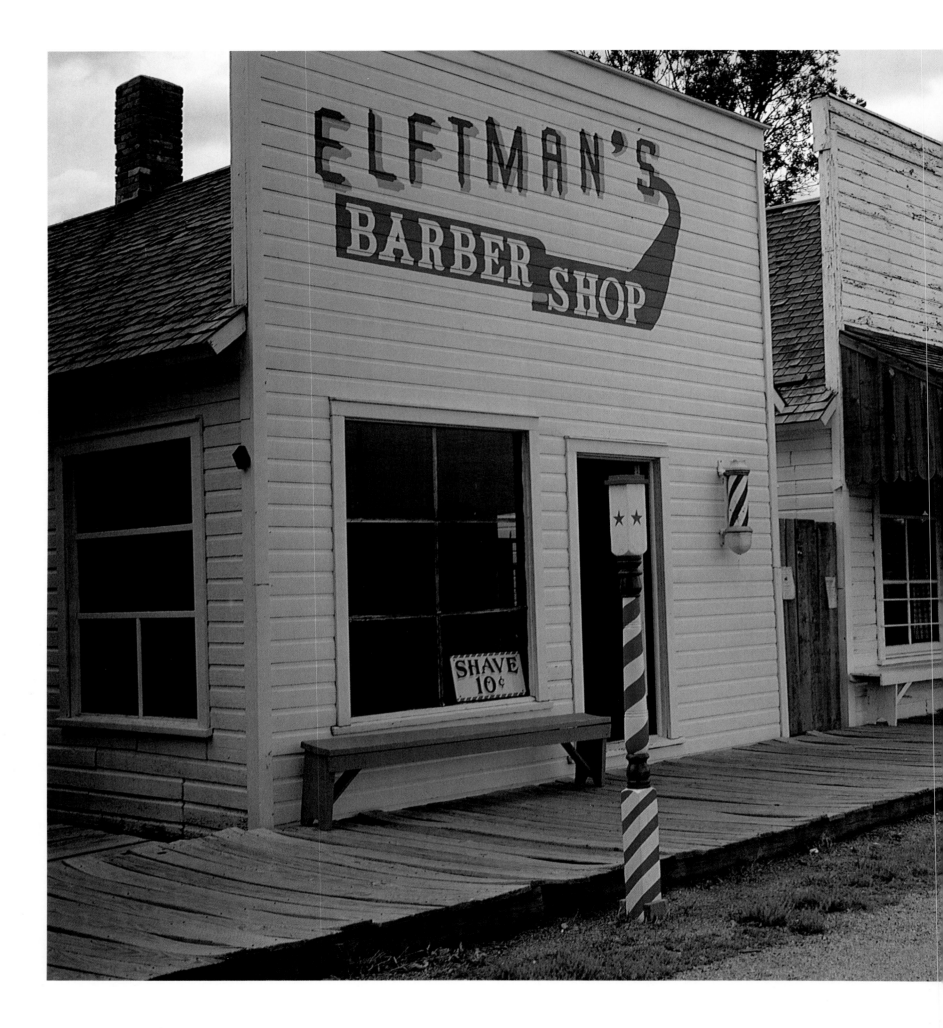

(*Left*) **Elftman's Barber Shop on Front Street and the bar next door represent two of the principal 19th-century establishments where men could gather to discuss crops and politics.**

(*Below*) **This seamstress puts the finishing touches on a 19th-century bonnet. Examples of her lovely handiwork hang behind her.**

In addition to the railroad town, Stuhr also boasts a Pioneer Village. Its eight log cabins with open-hearth fireplaces bridge the architectural gap between sod buildings and later frame homes. Such cabins, dating from 1857 to 1867, were often called "road ranches" because westward-bound travelers along the Platte River Valley trail stopped at them to socialize and seek assistance. The Menck Cabin features hand-hewn logs dovetailed at the corners and a mixture of mud and grass filling the gaps between the logs. This type of construction was common in 1859 when one of the area's first settlers built the house. Inside are fine examples of tables, chests, cradles, and cooking utensils.

The lifestyle of the prairie pioneer may be compared with that of native Americans at the mound-like Pawnee Indian earth lodge, an above-ground structure covered with grassy earth that is furnished with duplicates of the pottery, clothing, tools, and weapons used by the Pawnees at the time of the early settlers' arrival. Pawnee villages included a number of such houses, each fortified and featuring a vegetable garden.

Stuhr Museum, operated by Hall County, was founded in 1960 when the late Leo B. Stuhr, a Grand Island businessman and history enthusiast, donated land and money for the project. Since then, government agencies, private enterprise, and individuals have cooperated to find, relocate, and restore historic buildings in order to create the multifaceted complex.

The main museum building, designed by renowned architect Edward Durrell Stone, is situated on a circular island surrounded by a moat. Its overhanding facades and columns reflect similar themes used by Stone in his design of the U.S. Embassy in New Delhi, India. Modular exhibits display furnishings, clothing, tools, and gadgets, while an audio-visual presentation, "Land of the Prairie Pioneer," narrated by actor Henry Fonda, depicts the period between 1850 and 1900 in Nebraska. Fonda was born in a small 1883 frame bungalow in Grand Island in 1905. At his behest, the home was relocated and restored as part of the musuem complex, with furnishings based on old family photographs. He also recorded a commentary on his family history.

An important donation to the museum was Gus Fonner's large collection of Old West and Plains Indian artifacts, which contrast the lifestyle of the early settlers and the Plains Indians. The collecton is now housed in the Gus Fonner Memorial Rotunda south of the main museum.

One of the most pleasant ways to tour the museum complex is aboard the Nebraska Midland Railroad train. Its steam-powered engine—Old No. 69—with its bell clanging and whistle screaming, pulls an 1872 coach slowly through the 200-acre complex as part of the living history interpretation conducted from May through September.

(*Above right*) **The Danish Lutheran Church at the Stuhr Museum boasts a decorative spire which is a symbol of the 1888 structure.**

(*Right*) **A conductor waves the all clear for a ride around the 200-acre Stuhr Museum in an 1872 passenger car.**

THE INDIAN WARS

Early conflicts between native Americans and the white settlers generally were cultural in nature as well as territorial. Concepts of right and wrong differed. So did notions of the ownership of property and the codes of warfare. While the Indians quickly recognized the threat posed by the white settlers, they did not know how to respond to their perception. Initially, they chose to trade with the newcomers. While they welcomed the weapons, clothing, and food they received for surplus buffalo hides and furs, contact with whites also introduced them to the debilitating effect of whiskey and the deadly effect of European diseases such as measles, against which they had no immunity.

The sporadic conflicts between whites and Indians early in the 19th century gave way to steady warfare by the 1840s, as wagon trains became commonplace along the Santa Fe Trail, which opened in 1831, and the Oregon Trail, which opened at the end of the 1830s. The increasing number of settlers and transients ruined the pastureland, cut valuable trees, and slaughtered the large buffalo herds on which the Plains Indians' existence depended. The native Americans felt menaced by permanent white settlements in their traditional lands and stagecoach routes through them.

And so the Indian Wars began. They were marked by a series of long campaigns, many small skirmishes, and more than 200 battles as part of scattered uprisings, raids, ambushes, massacres, punitive search-and-destroy expeditions, narrow escapes, evasions, and long-range cavalry patrols. The battleground extended from the Canadian border to the Southwest, as customary army tactics were altered to meet the Indian hit-and-run style of warfare. Gen. William Tecumseh Sherman of Civil War fame made this prediction when appointed general-in-

FORT LARAMIE

chief of the U.S. Army in 1869: "We have now provided reservations for all, off the main roads. All who cling to their old hunting grounds are hostile and will remain so till killed off. We will have a sort of predatory war for years—every now and then be shocked by the indiscriminate murder of travelers and settlers, but the country is so large, and the advantage of the Indians so great, that we cannot make a single war end it."

There was no unified Indian nation to stand against the great white threat. Ancient intertribal antagonisms sometimes made an alliance with the Americans seem the lesser of evils, a case of fearing the enemy one knows more than the enemy one does not know. The warlike Sioux were among the last tribes to submit to white domination of the northern Plains area, after their defeat at Wounded Knee, South Dakota, in 1890. Three years before Wounded Knee, Congress passed the

Dawes Act of 1887, which ended tribal autonomy and divided up reservation land, giving each family head 160 acres to farm. After a 25-year probationary period, he would be given full ownership and U.S. citizenship. (In 1934, all native Americans were granted citizenship.)

Unlike its depiction in most Western movies, the conquest of the Indians was due as much to advanced weapons and superior numbers as to differences in combat skills. One of the decisive elements in the conflict were the forts constructed at strategic locations throughout the West. The surviving structures continue to tell in vivid detail the story of their individual triumphs and tragedies in the larger context of the struggle.

Fort Laramie National Historic Site

As an area became more settled and the Indians departed for new wide-open spaces, the need for military protection diminished. Many western forts partook in a small way in the taming of the frontier. Fort Laramie near Guernsey, Wyoming, however, witnessed the full sweep of the West's conquest and settlement.

The fort began as a trading post for beaver fur and buffalo hide. In 1834, William Sublette and Robert Campbell, two traders, built a palisade on the Laramie River near its confluence with the Platte, southwest of the present town of Fort Laramie. Contemporary paintings by Alfred Jacob Miller show a number of tepees on a plain adjacent to the fort and an active Indian presence inside its walls. Trading expanded further after the American Fur Company acquired the post in 1836 and replaced its rotting timber walls with a new 15-foot-high log stockade. Fort John—its official name—was located about one-third the distance between Independence, Missouri, and the Far West destinations of the pioneer wagon trains, which made it a popular resting place along the exhausting Oregon Trail. Later it served as a stopping place for the Cheyenne–Deadwood stagecoach line to the goldfields of the Black Hills.

The army acquired the post in 1848 and used it as living quarters while constructing a new fort around a large parade ground. The ensuing 20 years saw a dramatic rise in Indian attacks as more and more whites moved into and through the area. In 1851, a peace council near Fort Laramie attended by 10,000 Indians attempted to resolve the differences between the races but produced an ineffective treaty. The "Grattan Massacre" in 1854 resulted in the deaths of Brev. 2nd Lt. John L. Grattan, an interpreter, and 29 infantrymen who were sent to a Sioux village to recover a cow believed to have been taken from a passing wagon train. Indian attacks increased as the discovery of gold and silver in Montana stimulated traffic on the Bozeman Trail, which crossed Sioux hunting grounds. An unproductive military campaign against the Indians in the 1860s, led by veteran Indian fighter Gen. Patrick Conner, ushered in a new attempt at conciliation. This, too, came to nothing when construction of new forts along the Bozeman Trail angered even moderate Indian chiefs.

Fort Laramie continued as a staging area for combat against the Indians well into the 1870s, but it was attacked only once, in 1864, when a band of Indians rode onto the parade ground and drove off a few horses. The army gave chase but never caught the thieves. Finally, the Indian War in Wyoming came to an end: the fort was closed in 1890, and 59 of its 60 buildings were sold at public auction.

Homesteaders purchased some of the buildings, thus saving them from destruction, but others were stripped of usable building materials and left untended. Handsome "Old Bedlam," built in 1849 as the bachelor officers' quarters and the oldest military building in Wyoming, was maintained for 30 years by the last post trader, John Hunton, but it was in bad condition when the State of Wyoming acquired it in the 1930s

(*Opposite*) **Many of the buildings at Fort Laramie, like these officers' quarters, deteriorated over time and are now in ruins.**

(*Below*) **The parade ground and cavalry barracks at Fort Laramie were bustling places indeed when the outpost protected prospectors and settlers traveling on the Bozeman Trail.**

and donated it to the federal government. Authentic restoration, so thorough that square cut nails and oak dowels were used, was begun by the National Park Service in 1938 and completed in 1963. Nearly a dozen other structures have been restored, re-creating their roles in the 1870s and 1880s.

Part of "Old Bedlam" continues to look like the bachelor officers' quarters it was around 1854/55, while the second half of the two-story white-frame structure is restored to its use in 1863/64 as the headquarters of Lt. Col. William O. Collins. The commandant and his wife lived on the second floor, and the room behind his office was the officers' mess. The name apparently derives from the parties thrown by bachelor officers during the early years.

The two-story lime-concrete Burt House was one of only two single-family houses on the post. It is furnished as it was in 1884, when Lt. Col. Andrew Sheridan Burt lived there with his family on his second tour of duty at the fort. Information about the decor from Reynolds Burt, who lived there as a youth, and the donation of some of the original household items helped in achieving the authenticity of the restoration. The Captain's Quarters, in a duplex building, contain furnishings of the 1870s (such furniture was more readily available after the railroad reached Cheyenne in 1867). The lime-concrete Post Surgeon's Quarters of 1875, also in a duplex building, are furnished in the Victorian style of the early 1880s, with ornate chairs, low-hanging table coverings, and window drapes. An Apache water jar and other items in the study-office suggest that the surgeon saw service in the Southwest before his posting to Ft. Laramie. The long two-story enlisted men's cavalry barracks looks ready to accept new assignees.

A gun crew readies the post cannon for firing. Park rangers demonstrate the use of frontier artillery on a regular basis.

This room recreates the office of Lt. Col. William O. Sullivan, post commander in the early 1860s.

The Post Trader's Store and Complex, built in 1849 to house a civilian sutler licensed by the army, has been restored to its 1876 appearance. An 1883 addition housed an officers' club and a bar for enlisted men and civilians. The stone Magazine, constructed in 1850, has also been restored, as has the small 1876 Old Bakery with its two ovens capable of producing 500 loaves of bread per baking. The Old Guardhouse stands as it did in 1866, when guards occupied the second floor and the cells had no furniture, heat, or light for prisoners. The New Guardhouse from 1876 improved conditions somewhat. The 1884 Commissary Storehouse houses the Visitors Center, where audio-visual presentations review the history of the fort and related subjects and a small museum displays artifacts.

Walking tours of the complex are provided, along with living history interpretations of life at this military outpost, including its domestic side. The Old Bakery is still used on a regular basis to demonstrate the making of a primary staple in the soldier's diet, the 20-ounce loaf of bread which was accompanied by a 1-pound slab of pork or beef and "enough coffee to wash it down."

Fort Davis National Historic Site

FORT DAVIS, TEXAS

After the Republic of Texas joined the Union in 1845 and New Mexico and California were ceded to the United States by Mexico, a steady stream of settlers made their way through the Southwest along a variety of routes.

The Apaches (ranging from central Texas to Arizona) and Comanches (in eastern Colorado and later northwest Texas) were unreconciled to such intrusions into their traditional lands, intrusions which rose dramatically after the discovery of gold in California. Frequent attacks against migrants and stagecoaches, as well as mail and freight wagons, were facilitated by a traditional Comanche war trail to Mexico which intersected the El Paso Road. Fort Davis was constructed in response to this threat. It was the largest and most important of a string of forts in West Texas and, for almost 40 years, played an important role in the history of the southwestern frontier.

In 1854, Gen. Persifor F. Smith, commander of the Department of Texas, personally selected the first site of the fort in a box canyon near the Davis Mountains because water, wood, and grass were available nearby. He named the post for President Franklin Pierce's Secretary of War, Jefferson Davis, a West Point graduate who championed western forts and was an innovator in the development of tactics, including the military use of camels.

The first contingent assigned to the fort was the 8th U.S. Infantry under Lt. Col. Washington Seawell. As Seawell super-

vised construction of temporary pine slab buildings, he envisioned a stronger, more permanent fort near the entrance of the canyon. While six stone barracks were later erected across the mouth of the canyon, obstreperous Indians—and the attendant need to guard mail carriers and supply trains—kept Colonel Seawell from building a new structure. The fort was evacuated early in the Civil War, and Confederate forces used it as a staging area for the invasion of the New Mexico Territory. They abandoned the fort after that invasion proved unsuccessful. Thereafter, it remained idle for five years, during which it was vandalized and burned by Indians. When the post was rebuilt in June 1867, it boasted a more substantial structure with large adobe outposts constructed by the new commandant, Lt. Col. Wesley Merritt, near the site advocated by Seawell.

From 1867 to 1885, the post was garrisoned primarily by the black soldiers of the 9th and 10th U.S. Cavalry and the 24th and 25th U.S. Infantry Regiments. Commanded by white officers, the black soldiers joined the 1879/80 campaign against the great Apache chief Victorio, during which Col. Benjamin H. Grierson, commander of Fort Concho, established his head-

A "trooper" approaches Fort Davis, the outpost which guarded the San Antonio-El Paso road against Indian attack from 1854 to 1891. In the distance, one can see the ruins of the officers' quarters.

quarters at Davis. In one key action during the summer of 1880, Victorio's band was ambushed at the Tinaja de las Palmas waterhole 60 miles northwest of the fort. Victorio was ultimately driven back across the border into Mexico, where he was killed in a clash with Mexican soldiers.

Indian warfare in West Texas virtually ceased with the death of Victorio, and the daily routine at the post was enlivened only by occasional bandit chases, border patrols, and escort duty. By the time the fort was abandoned in 1891, more than 60 adobe and stone buildings, the last of which were built in the 1880s, provided a relatively comfortable life for a complement of up to 600 men.

The reassuring presence of the fort stimulated settlement of the region, including the still-functioning town of Fort Davis to service the military garrison. The town also became a center for the ranching industry as it grew to maturity in the 1880s under the fort's protection.

(*Above*) **This "trooper" relaxes while waiting for assembly. At Fort Davis, bugle calls mark the events of the day, as they did when the fort was in service.**

(*Left*) **The post commissary was a vital place at Fort Davis for here were stored the rations, including meat, bread, and coffee, that the United States army provided for each soldier.**

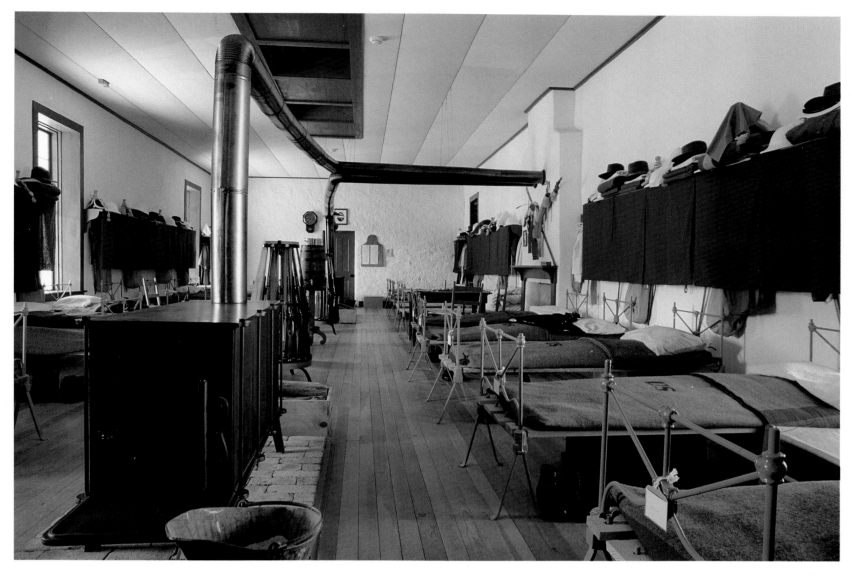

As this reconstructed barracks illustrates, the quarters for enlisted men at Fort Davis were comfortable and airy, compared to those of many other western forts.

Resurrection of this outstanding example of a southwestern frontier military post was initiated in the early 1950s by the inhabitants of the town of Fort Davis. Declared a National Historic Site in 1961, the 460-acre location was acquired by the National Park Service. A two-year restoration and preservation program preceded Fort Davis's opening to the public in 1966. Restoration of 25 structures and stabilization of dozens of ruins were aimed at providing a vivid impression of life during the fort's heyday.

Fort Davis is not a walled outpost. It consists of orderly rows of permanent structures, including an impressive Officers' Row with large single-family residences and multiunit quarters for bachelor officers. These residences, furnished appropriately for the period, are among the structures open to visitors. Others include barracks for enlisted men, warehouses, a magazine, the hospital, and granary. One restored barracks houses a Visitors Center, a museum which displays many of the 18,000 relics of the period owned by the National Historic Site, and a slide program on the fort's history.

During the summer months, park rangers and volunteers in period dress represent officers, enlisted men, officers' wives, and servants. They are stationed at the Commanding Officer's Quarters, Enlisted Men's Barracks, and the kitchen area. Special programs include the Fourth of July celebration and the annual Restoration Festival over the Labor Day weekend, the latter sponsored by the Friends of Fort Davis National Historic Site, Inc., to raise funds for the ongoing restoration program.

Archeologists have discovered the foundations of the first fort (1854–1861) west of the main site and a Butterfield stage station to the southeast. In the town of Fort Davis, the Truehart House is of pioneer vintage and several adobe structures built in the 1800s remain. The longest unpaved stretch of the Overland Trail—about a mile in length—is located there.

THE RANCHER'S LIFE

While the military brought order to the wilderness, others brought civilization and thus gave order meaning. These were the men and women who claimed and settled the land, and made their claims stick despite Indian marauders and white renegades. Ranchers were among the first to give new purpose to the great expanses of plains and plateaus, helping to tame a region that would eventually become the states stretching from present-day Texas to present-day Montana.

Cattle ranching developed modestly in Texas during the 1840s and 1850s, but the great leap forward came during and after the Civil War with the exploitation of the vast grassy range of the northern plains. At first, the herds were small, almost lost in the vastness of the land, but the cattle thrived on the seemingly endless expanse of grass. Moreover, labor to manage the herds was cheap and cottonwood along the streams provided building materials. And so the industry thrived. Vast "cattle kingdoms" grew where land was measured not in acres or square miles but by the expanse one could see with the eye or the distance a horse could travel in a day or a week. By 1865, more than 5 million longhorns grazed on Texas range land, where they were targets for rustlers and unreconciled Indians.

The coming of the railroads made hungry markets in the East readily accessible to the cattle industry. The era when giant herds were driven to railroad terminals may be seen as the final phase of the Wild West, according to historian Samuel Eliot Morison. The great cattle drives across the open range began in late 1865, when the railroad reached Sedalia, Missouri. Joseph M. McCoy, an Illinois meat dealer who was the first to organize and coordinate the shipment of meat to Chicago, established Abilene, Texas, as his railhead, but the focus later moved back to Missouri. In Wyoming, Cheyenne and Laramie became cattle centers on the Union Pacific Railroad. Rails soon stretched into the rolling pastures of Montana as well. There, an estimated 67,000 cattle in 1867

THE NATIONAL RANCHING HERITAGE CENTER

grew to almost a million head by 1885, and would go even higher. By 1895, the 11 range states had an estimated total of 20.5 million head of cattle.

The first of the newcomers were often wild, rough, strong-willed individuals, sometimes heroic and sometimes tyrannical. Just as untamed were the towns they frequented. But as the ranching territories became more settled, the lands of the cattle barons were given legal boundaries. New ranches also developed, sometimes through the sale of stock certificates abroad, as well as in the United States. Finally, law and order replaced frontier justice. Thus, with the history of ranching of the latter half of the 19th century, one can trace the advance of civilization in the West and the development of America's heartland.

THE GRANT-KOHRS NATIONAL HISTORICAL SITE

The National Ranching Heritage Center

"Red Hog Rachel" is one of the immortals in the annals of Texas cattle ranching. Her fame rests solely on her unexplained association with an unknown cowhand, who spent a lonely night on the Texas plains burning her name into the log wall of a half-dugout building. Other cowboys left marks and personal thoughts on the building, too, but none are as intriguing as that tribute to Rachel.

The log building, circa 1891, partially embedded in a hill, is typical in construction of the temporary shelters erected on ranchlands where trees were scarce. It also illustrates the use of primitive structures as line or fence camps along ranch boundaries throughout the 19th century.

The dugout originally stood on the Matador Ranch in Dickens County, which ran about 50,00 head of cattle and was purchased in 1885 by a group of investors. Today it is one of more than 30 buildings at the 12-acre National Ranching Heritage Center at Lubbock, which despite its name focuses primarily on the ranching history of Texas. The structures, relocated from sites throughout the state, occupy re-created settings almost identical to those of the originals. The presentation is made more authentic by earthen berms which visually block out nearby modern development.

Through the structures it has gathered, the center traces cattle ranching from its humble beginnings in the early 1800s through the affluence that came with railroad access to eastern markets after the Civil War up to the dawn of the 20th century. It also provides outstanding examples of structures associated with the business of ranching, from the distant line shacks that protected cowboys far from the bunkhouse to the owner's ranch house and headquarters.

The oldest structure on the grounds is a log cabin which was built without windows in Gonzales County about 1838. Typical of the primitive log structures which housed the first big ranchers, it sheltered the owners of the El Capote Ranch during the period just after Texas became a republic. One of the owners was Michael Erskine, who pioneered trail herding by delivering 1000 head of cattle to California in 1853. Hedwig Hill Cabin, built about 1850, typifies the style favored by German immigrants who became ranchers. It features double log cabins, with a dogtrot between its wings to provide breezes in hot weather. The fine craftsmanship of these immigrants is evident in the cabin's furnishings, which include spinning wheels, butter molds, and carved wood chests.

The kind of improved living conditions that accompanied the post–Civil War cattle boom can be found at a number of the center's homes, including the July House, of stone, circa 1875, which replaced a cattleman's log cabin reputedly burned by Indians while its owner was on a trail drive to Kansas; the large and prestigious Harrell House, which grew from a one-room stone structure, circa 1883; and the Victorian-style Barton House, constructed in 1909 at Abernathy. The last includes innovations rare for ranch houses even at the turn of the century: running water, two indoor bathrooms, and large closets. Materials for the house were hauled 100 miles by wagon. Of course, not everyone could afford such a luxury; the Pickett and Sotol House, built around 1904 to "prove up" a homestead near Ozona, Texas, has walls made of cedar pickets and sotol stalks, as well as a thatched roof.

Texas Tech students lead children in 19th-century games at the National Ranching Heritage Center, in Lubbock, Texas.

Other structures—those associated with the business side of ranching—are in evidence at the center as well. There is a cattleman's office, built around 1880 for the Matador Ranch; the Masterson Bunkhouse, built around the mid-1800s for the cowhands of the JY Ranch in King County; and the Reynolds–Gentry Barn, circa 1877, with its six stalls, two feed rooms, a tack room, and a hayloft.

The railroad's importance to ranching is illustrated by the Fort Worth & Denver steam engine, built by Baldwin Locomotive Works in 1923, and the Santa Fe livestock cars and caboose, as well as several historical railroad buildings. The rail car house, circa 1917, and the 1918 station from Ropesville stand near cattle shipping pens once owned by the King Ranch.

The one-room schoolhouse, which dates from the late 1890s, illustrates the attempt to provide education even among scattered ranches. It was moved from one spread to another, finally resting on the C. A. Barfield Ranch in Donley County, but remained in use until 1937. A single teacher taught all the grades.

From time to time, guides at the center, which is operated by Texas Tech University, illustrate the near self-sufficiency of the rancher's life during the 19th century. They shoe horses, shear sheep, bake sourdough bread, and churn butter. Orientation programs are given in the David M. DeVitt and Mallet Ranch Building. The displays include wagons, saddles, branding irons, and Western art.

(*Right*) **Host Doug Williams, seated on the porch of the Hedwig Hill cabin, enjoys demonstrating the way to make a gourd dipper.**

(*Opposite*) **The hallway of the Harrell House gives entrance to the south bedroom, which was added to the house around 1930. The building was donated to the center by the Harrell sisters from Snyder, Texas in 1972.**

(*Below*) **The stone Jowell House seems well designed to survive the deep snow and harsh winds of a north Texas winter.**

Grant–Kohrs Ranch National Historic Site

Most Americans today don't realize how vast Western cattle ranches were in their heyday. Modern spreads, even those that stretch as far as the eye can see, would have been dwarfed by some of the empires that developed from a few emaciated cows during the latter half of the 19th century. The Grant–Kohrs Ranch near Deer Lodge, Montana, was one of them.

When John Francis (Johnny) Grant, a Canadian trapper and hunter for Hudson's Bay Company, decided to settle down in Montana's fertile Deer Lodge Valley in 1862, he purchased a few head of cattle from migrants on the Oregon Trail. Soon, he was one of the leading ranchers in Montana. To build his herd, he developed the practice of trading one of his rested, well-fed cows to passersby for a couple of trail-worn cattle, a fair swap considering that many of the travelers—and their stock—still had a considerable journey ahead of them. In 1862, Grant moved his operation to a site near Deer Lodge in the heart of the great, unfenced open range of western Montana. There, he built a two-story log house with 28 windows and green shutters, described in one newspaper article as the finest house in Montana. Grant lived there with his wife, Quarra, a Bannock Indian, and their large family. A contemporary sketch shows an imposing structure with its yard enclosed by a jacklegged fence. An Indian tepee in the yard illustrates the ranch's secondary role, that of an Indian trading post. By the time Grant decided to sell out and return to Canada in 1866, he owned more than 2000 head of cattle. The inventory of other items—his furniture, sheep, goats, hay, and grain—showed that his ranch was a large and profitable operation.

The new owner was a German immigrant, Conrad Kohrs, who had tried gold mining before earning a reputation as a butcher and shrewd beef trader. Kohrs already owned a sizable herd by the time he purchased Grant's land and buildings; now, in partnership with his half brother, John Bielenberg, he built his new holdings into a small empire. Indeed, by the turn of the century, the ranch covered more than 25,000 acres and its operations extended across a million acres of land in three states and Canada. Kohrs owned some 30,000 to 50,000 cattle and at least 1000 horses and was one of the most prominent men in the West. He was a founder of the Montana Stockgrowers Association and a member of the territorial and state legislatures.

The Grant–Kohrs National Historic Site was set aside in 1972 by Act of Congress "to provide an understanding of the frontier cattle era of the nation's history, to preserve the Grant–Kohrs Ranch, and to interpret the nationally significant values thereof for the benefit and inspiration of the present and future generations." Thirty-four historic buildings and 19 other structures on a 265-acre site fulfill this mission, interpreting life on a working ranch from the mid-1850s through the present day. The structures and their interpretation evoke the pioneering spirit of the determined, hardworking people who risked physical hardship and deprivation, isolation, famine, disease, and harsh weather to make a stubborn land produce.

The park site straddles the tracks of the Chicago, Milwaukee, St. Paul & Pacific Railroad tracks, with the Visitors Center on one side and the ranch complex on the other. A railroad underpass connects the two.

This 23-room ranch house was built in two sections and altered several times. The first unit dates from 1862.

(*Above*) A ranch hand spruces up in the bunkroom at Grant-Kohrs Ranch, founded in 1862 when vast areas of Montana were open range.

(*Right*) Many of the fine furnishings in the parlor of the Grant-Kohrs Ranch house were acquired by Augusta Kohrs, wife of the second owner.

As with many frontier buildings that were improved and enlarged over time, the 23-room main ranchhouse was built in two sections: the log main section in 1862 by Grant, and a frame and brick addition in 1889 by Kohrs. Bunkhouse row, where the cowboys and other ranchhands lived and ate, also changed a number of times from the log structure that Grant erected in about 1860. The furnishings in both the ranchhouse and bunkhouse are original to the site, with many of the items in the former acquired by Kohrs's wife, Augusta, who came to the territory as a bride of 19.

Most of the ancillary buildings erected on the ranch prior to 1885 have simple log walls. These structures include the 1880s ice house, where ice cut in winter was stored under sawdust for summer use; a frame lean-to was added later as the summer bedroom of the Chinese cook. Also made of logs are the 1870 oxen barn and the Leeds Lion stallion barn, built around 1885 and named for a famous Shire owned by Kohrs. The 1885 thoroughbred barn, first used as a stable and then as a show barn, is a frame building. It now houses a large assortment of horse-drawn vehicles and farm machinery.

The Visitors Center is large enough to display only a few of the 12,000 historical relics owned by the park. Others are on view at some of the buildings, but many are simply in storage. The archives hold thousands of old photos depicting life on the ranch and in Montana during the 19th and early 20th centuries.

Visitors may wish to enjoy some of the simple pleasures that 19th-century folks enjoyed, such as fishing in the Clark River or strolling along the rustic roads, or just lolling under the shade trees or on the creekbank. Guided walking tours, led by park rangers, are supplemented by interpretive demonstrations depicting ranch activities, such as use of horse- and ox-drawn equipment and blacksmithing.

The buildings at the Grant-Kohrs Ranch include the lower buggy shed in the foreground with the stallion barn and blacksmith shop (now used for storage) in the distance.

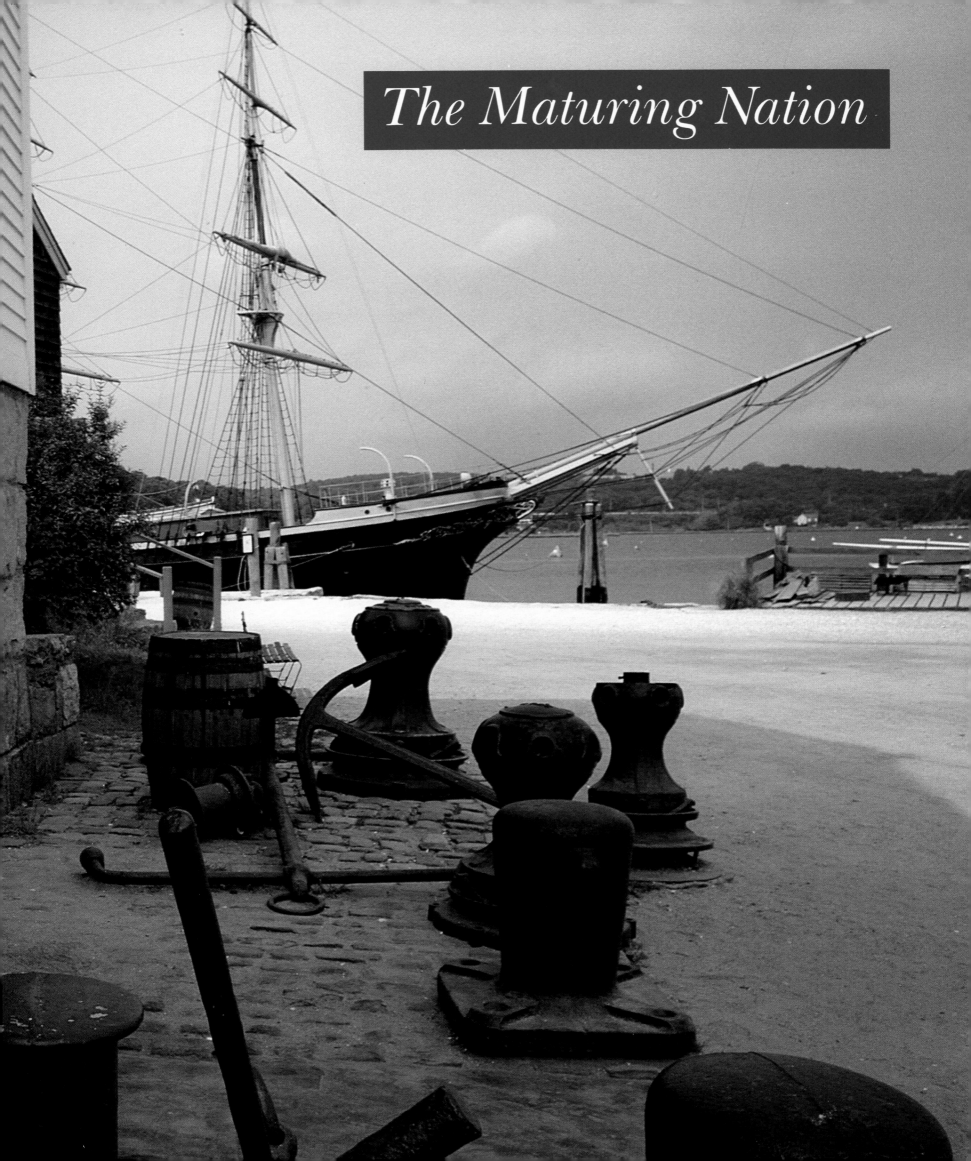

THE SHELBURNE MUSEUM

BELCOURT CASTLE, NEWPORT, R.I.

The vigor that had propelled the United States since its colonization in the 17th century reached a fever pitch as the 20th century approached. Although the post–Civil War period was a time of great expansion—marked by a transportation–communications revolution—there were some setbacks such as the Wall Street Panics of 1873 and 1893, each of which led to sharp periods of business recession. Such slumps gave powerful financiers like J. P. Morgan opportunities to expand their holdings at bargain prices.

While many citizens at the time may not have noticed the signposts of America's coming of age, the evidence in retrospect is quite apparent. Agriculture, the basis of all economic systems, produced an abundance of goods. A mass migration from the farms to the cities—slow at first but gathering momentum as the century progressed—supplied the manpower demanded first by the industrial revolution and later by that American innovation, mass production. The electric light and typewriter made

(*Preceeding pages*) **Ship chandleries, like this New England version at Mystic Seaport in Connecticut, were a familiar site in port cities around the world.**

business more efficient. Coal, iron, and copper were among the abundant raw materials wrested from the land. By 1890, U.S. steel production alone passed 4 million tons a year. Shipbuilding, both for the merchant fleet and the U.S. Navy, was booming.

Newspapers engaged in circulation wars and occasionally took on politics as well. The "yellow" press even helped to precipitate a "splendid little war," as Secretary of State John Hay dubbed the brief but decisive Spanish-American conflict of 1898. Politics was dominated to a large extent by the demands of trade, abroad as well as at home.

The American urge to trade and travel had a dramatic impact on those who plied the sea. American merchant and passenger ships roamed the world, opening new ports of call in exotic, faraway places. In 1898, the United States annexed the Hawaiian Islands, and America was on its way to its new role as a global power.

Lifestyles changed, too. An abundance of goods at relatively cheap prices created a growing demand that would become a tidal wave of consumption as the 20th century advanced. New

processes were developed for refining petroleum, destined to become a primary source of energy, and numerous ways to use it were discovered by the growing petrochemical industry. Homes were equipped with revolutionary electrical fixtures, including home refrigeration. And new forms of entertainment, such as the phonograph and motion picture, and advanced systems of communication, such as the telegraph and telephone, brought families closer together and the world closer to home.

During this period, dubbed the "Gilded Age," a few Americans, including J. P. Morgan, Cornelius Vanderbilt, and John D. Rockefeller, achieved great wealth and formed a powerful elite, the Four Hundred, mostly concentrated in the Northeast, especially New York City. They built mansions and summer "cottages" that rivaled the splendor of Europe's palaces, and they traveled in the comfort of their own private railroad cars and yachts.

This transitional era, the period when America evolved to a world power, is vividly preserved at several sites in the Northeast. Among them are Mystic Seaport, the Shelburne Museum, and Newport, Rhode Island.

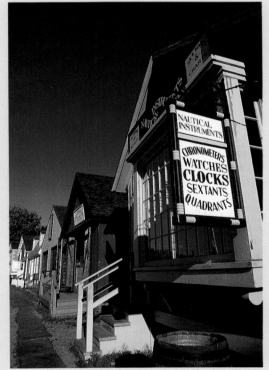

MYSTIC SEAPORT

Mystic Seaport Museum

In any New England coastal village, the ships and boats are not only the center of attention for the passerby, who may spend many happy hours watching them get under way, they are the economic heart of the community.

Seagoing vessels are among the principal attractions as well at Mystic Seaport, a re-created, 17-acre village in Mystic, Connecticut, where more than 300 watercraft—the largest collection in the United States and one of the largest collections in the world—await inspection. Ship buffs, at least, head for these first. So do many children, who fancy themselves as captains or able-bodied seamen as they look over the hulls, walk the decks, or sail on the Mystic River.

Perhaps the most notable of the village's historic New England vessels is the 113-foot, 11-inch *Charles W. Morgan*, launched in 1841 at New Bedford, Massachusetts. The vessel, which is the only surviving American wooden whaleship, is a registered national landmark. A tour of its two decks and the cargo hold illustrates the cramped but serviceable conditions under which sailors lived on voyages that lasted as long as five years. A tour starts on the main deck, where in the "round house" (or afterdeck house) one finds the galley (or kitchen). On the lower deck are the captain's quarters, complete with a swinging berth which Capt. Tom Landers installed in 1864 to entice his wife to make a voyage; berths of the chief, second, and third mates; the officers' mess with a built-in table; quarters for the fourth mate; and steerage. Above the hold is the blubber room, where barrels of whale oil were stored. The crew's quarters in the forecastle are now used as a workspace for restoration and repair work. The visitor emerges from the forward hatch near brick try-pots that were used to extract oil from blubber.

Near the *Charles W. Morgan* is the 123-foot schooner *L. A. Dunton*, built in 1921. This Gloucester-style boat, commonly used for fishing on the Grand Banks, invites visitors to walk the deck under its two tall masts and go below to the crew's quarters. Also moored at the village docks is the last coal-fired steamboat still running in the United States, the 1908 *Sabino* built in East Boothbay, Maine, which still makes passenger runs on the Mystic River on a regular schedule between May and October.

The boats are manned by costumed sailors. It is particularly exciting to see them climb the rope rigging of the tall ships, the equivalent of scaling a 7-story building, and to watch them set and furl sails.

A number of smaller vessels also are tied to the village's wharves and docks. Among them are the 46-foot Noank fishing smack *Emma C. Berry*, the 34-foot Maine sloop *Estrella A*, and the oyster sloop *Nellie*.

Visitors are welcome at the Henry B. duPont Preservation Shipyard, where they can observe skilled craftsmen engaged in the preservation of older vessels using methods employed during the latter half of the 19th century.

The concentration of vessels at the Seaport is appropriate, for the village of Mystic was a major shipbuilding center until the 1870s. Its yards produced some of the fastest clippers to sail the oceans of the world, including the *David Crockett*, which made more than 25 runs around Cape Horn to San Francisco. In fact, Mystic Seaport stands on the site of the George Greenman & Co. shipyard, where the *Crockett* was built.

Taverns like the Spouter were a mainstay of port life in the 19th century. The name pays homage to New England's premier role as the base for whalers.

Mystic Seaport displays an array of objects handcrafted by shipcarvers. Today such objects are highly regarded among collectors of American folk art.

(*Above*) With such simple tools, shipcarvers turned out a host of useful maritime objects, as well as many pieces endowed with ornamental beauty.

(*Right*) The iron-hulled *Joseph Conrad*, built in Denmark in 1882, is the site of Mystic Seaport's sail-training program.

While the fleet is an important part of Mystic's program, it is by no means the museum's only attraction. Rather, the boats are part of an authentic 19th-century coastal village, with more than 60 historic buildings, including an 1833 bank, an 1870s drygoods and hardware store, and an 1880s one-room schoolhouse. A rope walk, a sail loft, a ship chandlery, and other maritime crafts shops stand as testaments to the town's principal industry—fishing. The village also boasts several residences, all furnished in fashions appropriate to the second half of the 19th century and in a manner that represents the socioeconomic status of their owners. In addition, there are a number of exhibition areas, including the Stillman Building which houses a large and varied collection of scrimshaw and ship models; the Schaefer Building, which offers maritime art exhibits; and the Children's Museum, which features 19th-century toys and games.

The streets and shops of Mystic bustle with the activities of costumed interpreters. A carpenter labors over a mast. The woodcarver and storekeeper take time out from their work to discuss their daily lives and recent whaling news. Barrelmakers, blacksmiths, and printers turn out their wares. Aromas emanate from the 1830s Buckingham House when cooking is under way, while in the Edmondson House a weaver works his loom. Children roll hoops and walk on stilts on the lawns and streets. Sailors sing sea chanteys. And a horse-drawn carriage moves down a street, carrying passengers.

Christmas is special at Mystic as evergreen trees are tied to ships' masts and the sounds of storytelling and singing mix with the jingle of harness bells. In buildings decorated with wreaths, costumed interpreters talk with visitors about their preparations for the holiday, while on Lantern Light and Yuletide Light Tours, visitors pop into such places as a tavern where sailors are making merry and a home where a family is observing the holiday. Other annual events include a Lobster Festival in late May, a Sea Music Festival in mid-June, and a schooner race and chowderfest in early October.

The Seaport was conceived in 1929 by three Mystic residents—Dr. Charles K. Stillman, Edward E. Bradley, and Carl C. Cutler—who formed the Marine Historical Association, Inc., to acquire and assemble ships, historic structures, and artifacts that would preserve New England's maritime tradition. The name was changed to Mystic Seaport, Inc., in 1974 and to the Mystic Seaport Museum, Inc., in 1978. A respected research library is part of the complex.

The rigging of the *Charles W. Morgan*, the only wooden survivor of the era when New England whalers dominated the seas, provides a bird's-eye view of the orderly streets of Mystic Seaport.

Shelburne Museum

SHELBURNE, VERMONT

How many aspects of America's maturing life and character are portrayed at the Shelburne Museum? The list seems endless and includes both persistent and contrasting elements in the nation's cultural journey. Every building, every artifact, has a story—some have many stories—that reflect their use by real people at work or at play. Earlier in this volume, the museum's exhibits pertaining to the first half of the 19th century were explored (see *Part II: The Developing Nation, The Northeast*), but Shelburne's scope extends to the latter half of the century as well.

The round barn from 1901, for example, illustrates an effort to minimize the need for labor in New England from the post–Civil War era through at least World War I. During this period, the massive westward migration led to a shortage of farmhands in the East.

To pass the idle hours on whaling expeditions that sometimes lasted as long as five years, sailors used their knives and needles to create an art form on whale bones and teeth which became known as scrimshaw. Many of them carved gifts for loved ones back home: pie crimpers, sewing boxes, corset busks, knitting needles, and toys. Examples in the Shelburne Museum indicate a love of the sea, devotion to detail, and vivid imaginations.

Shelburne has the world's most extensive collection (nearly 1000) of waterfowl and shorebird decoys, exemplars of an everyday implement that evolved into a true art form. The collection shows how carvers developed styles to enhance their eye for detail and their understanding of form.

While blacksmithing declined as a trade late in the 19th century due to the mass production of implements and parts and the development of the automobile and power machinery, a smithy and wheelwright in the town of Shelburne managed to stay open until 1935. The shop was moved to the museum in 1956, where operation of the forge is demonstrated daily.

Of course, in the post–Civil War era, the arrival of a circus was a big event in any town. At Shelburne, a miniature circus parade, circa 1920, marches perpetually. The scale model (1 inch = 1 foot) representing a parade about 2 miles long, is the most extensive and accurate in existence. Stretching around the 518-foot wall of a horseshoe-shaped building especially designed to hold it are several thousand pieces, including 53 bandwagons, tableaux, and animal wagons, each colorfully

Dorset House at the Shelburne Museum is home to the world's most extensive collection of waterfowl and shorebird decoys.

The sidewheel of the S.S. *Ticonderoga*, **now on display at Shelburne Museum, churned the waters of the Great Lakes for many years.**

Turn-of-the-century women's hats and dresses are part of Shelburne's enormous collection of Americana.

decorated and accurate to the last detail. Wheels on the wagons, for example, measure only 2 inches yet are precise in shape and dimensions. Created by Roy Arnold of Springfield, Massachusetts, who enlisted the assistance of German wood-carvers, the model was begun in about 1925 and took 35 years to complete. Electra Webb, the museum's founder, purchased the circus parade in 1959.

Interesting comparisons between real and miniature objects can be made throughout the museum. For example, the last steam locomotive used on the Central Vermont Railroad—a giant Baldwin retired in the mid-1950s—stands in contrast to wood, tin, and cast iron transportation toys, including trains of

the 19th century, berthed at the Shelburne toy shop. Dollhouse kitchens can be examined in light of the real thing in the museum's vintage homes.

In forming her vast collection, Electra Webb let no impediment stand in the way. A case in point is the S.S. *Ticonderoga* (the "Ti"), which was scheduled to be scrapped in 1953. The 900-ton vessel was moved 2 miles from Shelburne Bay to the museum over railroad tracks laid solely for the move. The undertaking was started in winter, when 2–3 feet of ground frost was expected to support the ship's weight, but an early thaw caused some anxious moments. Tons of mud were removed from beneath the tracks to prevent the vessel from capsizing. In all, it took 65 days for the *Ticonderoga* to complete its final voyage. Now, it has been restored to its glory period—it began sailing on Lake Champlain in 1906—when passengers lounged in velvet sofas and chairs in the grand salon and strolled its freshly painted decks. As a complement to this massive exhibit, the museum also has numerous steamship relics and models.

The dining room from Electra Havemeyer Webb's New York apartment (featuring two paintings by Claude Monet) is one of six rooms installed in Shelburne's Memorial Building to honor the museum's founder.

Round barns—such as this one at Shelburne dating from 1901—were born of necessity as farmers strove to overcome a shortage of ready labor.

Newport Mansions

The name Newport conjures up images of palatial mansions populated with the families of wealthy tycoons. Indeed, the Gilded Age saw this sleepy New England town emerge as the nation's premiere playground of the rich and famous.

But the Rhode Island seaport was a recognized resort long before the late 19th century. Newport's founding fathers, a small group of people seeking religious freedom in 1638, indirectly helped turn the city into a resort even during the colonial period. The mix of early citizens—Quakers, Baptists, Jews, and others—produced a vibrant culture that joined with the appealing summer climate to attract erudite men and women, including scientific researchers, and vacationers to the tip of Aquidneck Island. Before the Revolutionary War, Newport was also a bustling seaport, one of the busiest in the colonies. Although its role as a commercial center declined during the first half of the 19th century, it remained a popular resort until the Civil War. After the war, the resort community recovered quickly, riding the crest of an industrial boom that swept the North and created a new social elite. Large hotels, catering to Boston businessmen and their families, emerged along with rows of waterfront cottages that played host to middle-class guests. Newport visitors spent money freely—a measure of breeding and respectability during the Gilded Age—and started the resort on the way to a reputation for palatial living.

The migration of wealthy financiers and industrialists from New York began about 1888. They created a close, competitive society, where being "somebody" meant lavishly demonstrating one's wealth. What emerged from these pecking contests among Astors, Vanderbilts, and their peers were palatial marble and granite mansions on large estates that freely mimicked European architecture. Ancillary buildings—even stables—were finer than the homes of many Americans. The Newport elite spent money extravagantly on yachts, interior decoration, art, landscaping and gardens, clothing, jewelry, fabulous parties, and even toys. Wives were often the social arbiters, spending huge sums to establish and maintain their bona fides. Life was a revolving series of dinners, luncheons, teas, cotillions, concerts, musical soirées featuring famous performers, and cruises on expensive yachts. "Conspicuous consumption" was the phrase coined by sociologist Thorstein Veblen to characterize life among Newport society, a phrase that continues in use today but refers to far less lavish displays of wealth.

Newport's golden age lasted little more than a generation, as great fortunes in other parts of the country—fostered by inventions such as the automobile—led to a diffusion of elite vacation spots. Moreover, New York's high society, the fabled "Four Hundred," turned to other resort communities on nearby Long Island and on Jekyll Island, Georgia. But the imprint of the Gilded Age on Newport is lasting and can still be seen in mansions along Ocean Drive, Ochre Point Avenue, and Bellevue Avenue.

The earliest of the extant mansions open to public view is Kingscote, an early-Victorian house built in 1839 for a wealthy Georgian plantation owner and enlarged in 1881 by Sanford White for then-owner David King, a former merchant in the China trade. Architect Richard Upjohn's original design makes harmonious use of various shapes, exterior decorations, and cutwork molding in a delightful rustic version of the Gothic

The ballroom at Belcourt Castle resembles a medieval fortress with Gothic arches and furniture, hanging banners, and suits of armor.

revival style. The interiors feature rich wood paneling and a stained-glass Tiffany window.

The Marble House, designed by architect Richard Morris Hunt and completed in 1892 for William K. Vanderbilt—one of the grandsons of the Commodore—illustrates the semantic misuse of the word "cottage" to describe the summer palaces of the rich at Newport. Some rooms are marble with gold trimming on the pilasters and ceilings, but the disparate elements create an opulent yet harmonious decor. The grandest room is the ballroom. It is the most sumptuous such room in Newport, boasting a large ceiling mural, carved and gilded woodwork, and an immense marble fireplace flanked by nearly life-size bronze statues of Youth and Old Age. The handsomely landscaped grounds are capped by a 1913/14 Chinese-style teahouse which has recently been restored.

At a cost of $11 million, Marble House set a new standard of opulence for Newport. It was a 39th birthday present from William to his wife Alva, who used the "cottage" to move into the first tier of Newport society, over the protests of the then-reigning queen, Mrs. William Blackstone Astor. When the Vanderbilts divorced in 1895, Alva kept her present as part of the settlement. But she soon spent her summers across the street at the "cottage" of her second husband, Oliver Hazard Perry Belmont.

The centerpiece of William K. Vanderbilt's Marble House is this ornate ballroom. The "cottage" took nearly four years and $11 million to build.

Called Belcourt Castle, it was completed in 1894 and modeled after a hunting lodge of Louis XIII of France. Today, the house is privately owned, but the main rooms are open for guided tours. These tours cover many of the owners' splendid collection of paintings, objets d'art, stained glass, fabrics, and antiques from 33 countries, including a golden coronation coach. By the way, Alma moved back to her previous summer home, Marble House, in 1908, after the death of August Belmont. But in the meantime, her former in-laws, William's brother Cornelius II and Alice, his wife, had built an even more spectacular Newport mansion, The Breakers.

The Breakers, which overlooks the Atlantic Ocean and Cliff Walk, became the grandest Newport mansion of all when it was completed by architect Richard Morris Hunt in 1895. The 72-room Italian marble "cottage" resembes a northern Italian Renaissance palace, complete with a central courtyard. Among the key features are an 18th-century reception room, ornate dining room, and elegant great hall. There is lavish interior use of alabaster, marble, and mosaics. The furnishings are original to the home. The grounds were landscaped by the famous New York firm headed by Frederick Law Olmstead (designer of Central Park). Adjacent to the house is a quaint Victorian cottage

that served as a playhouse for the children. The Breakers' stable on Coggeshall Avenue displays a large collection of carriages, coaches, and equestrian and livery equipment owned by the family.

The most recent of the grand Newport mansions open to the public is Rosecliff, built in 1902 for Mrs. Hermann Oelrichs. Architect Sanford White used the Grand Trianon at Versailles as his model for the house's impressive terra-cotta facade with Ionic columns. The 40-room interior features a curving marble staircase, a profuse use of molded plaster, and a bright, sumptuously decorated ballroom well suited to entertaining in the grand style. Part of the movie *The Great Gatsby* was filmed at this mansion.

Many other structures from Newport's early period as a resort and port city are still intact, including the handsome Hunter House on Washington Street, built in 1748 for a sea-trade merchant. Like several of the mansions of the Gilded Age, it was restored and is maintained by the Preservation Society of Newport County. Bowen' Wharf on Thames Street was part of the original harbor. It is now the site of numerous restaurants and quaint stores. The reconstructed frigate *Rose*, a 24-gun British ship which blockaded the city in 1774, is tied up at nearby Banister's Wharf.

(*Left*) The Breakers, the 70-room mansion of Cornelius Vanderbilt II, was the most lavish home in Newport when it was completed in 1895. This east facade is famous for its double loggia.

(*Below*) This handsome teahouse was added to Marble House in 1913, after Mrs. Oliver Hazard Perry Belmont, the former Mrs. William K. Vanderbilt, became a leader of the woman's suffrage movement.

(Left) The gardens, outdoor sculpture and expansive lawns are the pride of The Elms, completed in 1901 by coal magnate Edward Julius Berwind.

(*Below*) Kingscote, one of the oldest summer cottages in Newport, was constructed in the pre-Civil War era when wealthy Southerners maintained homes there.

THE MIDWEST

THE HENRY FORD MUSEUM AND GREENFIELD VILLAGE

The Midwest came of age during the latter half of the 19th century by dint of down-to-earth labor and aggressive management. Major improvements in farm implements, which began with Cyrus H. McCormick's simple first mechanical reaper and proliferated into a host of labor-saving devices (such as Jerome Case's "groundhog" thresher, which evolved into the "combine," a machine for cutting and threshing wheat in the field). These devices greatly expanded the farmer's ability to produce.

Meanwhile, urban centers too were emerging. Chicago became a major city, founded on meat packing but expanding into many other industries. Settlements along the major transportation routes—the rivers, canals, and established trails—benefited from the great migration into the Plains states and beyond, whether for ranching, farming, or mining. New waves of immigrants, especially those from northern Europe, barely paused at the coast before moving inland, creating ethnic enclaves that persist to a certain degree in states like Wisconsin and Minnesota.

Like any pioneering society, the Midwest was vibrant, tending to be egalitarian and upwardly mobile. Its influence in the nation increased as Midwestern foliage grew thick on the nourishment of eastern roots. It was not by accident that most of the presidents during the latter half of the 19th century came from the central region of the nation. Indeed, the Gilded Age saw something of a shift in power from the "old" money of the Northeast to the new money of the Midwest.

But the Midwest of the late 19th century had a marked duality in personality. Its core was still in the farms and the small rural communities that dotted the landscape. These are represented by Old World Wisconsin at Eagle, the Living History Museum at Des Moines, Iowa, and Stonefield Village at Cassville, Wisconsin. But the region also served as a crucible for revolutionary technological changes; it produced innovations and inventions that moved the United States into the modern era. This influence may be felt at several of the region's open-air museums and is the particular focus of the Henry Ford Museum and Greenfield Village in Dearborn, Michigan.

LIVING HISTORY FARMS

STONEFIELD VILLAGE

Stonefield Village

The final decades of the 19th century were a productive period for Wisconsin. After exhaustion of the soil had caused a decline in Wisconsin wheat farming in the 1870s, farmers experimented with flax, hops, sugar beets, and even tobacco before settling on a diversified menu of crops. The state also boasted ample pasture grasses and meadow hay to support dairy farming. Cheesemaking became a major industry. Soon villages and towns dotted the landscape, so that the farmer had to travel only 3 miles on average to reach the nearest town. These farms reflected a considerable degree of commercial specialization and integration into the national economy. They were becoming more sophisticated, too, as farmers and inventors developed new farm labor- and time-saving devices, such as the self-rake reaper, the mowing machine, and the seeder.

This vibrant and prosperous period comes alive in all its glory at Stonefield Village and related attractions at Cassville, Wisconsin. The 700-acre site has three distinct features: the village; the State Agricultural Museum; and the two-story Victorian mansion rebuilt in the 1870s by Wisconsin's first governor, Nelson Dewey, a lawyer and businessman who was also one of Wisconsin's leading gentlemen-farmers. Stonefield is named for his 2000-acre farm. Although the re-created village never existed as such, it combines historic and reconstructed buildings and relics to form a community typical of the hundreds that catered to farmers in southern Wisconsin in the 1890s.

The Visitors Center provides entrée to the village and to the agricultural museum. The latter uses dioramas and exhibits, audio-visuals, and exhibits of antique farm equipment to show what farm life was like at the close of the 19th century.

The path from the Visitors Center into the village passes the cheese factory and railroad depot. The proximity of these buildings is not incidental. Many of the men and women who settled in Wisconsin in the late 19th century brought with them a familiarity with animal husbandry and the processing of milk into cheese, butter, and other by-products that gave the state's agricultural industry a boost. Railroads, which had ready access to urban markets and farm supplies, turned these products into profitable cash crops.

A 50-foot covered bridge, built in 1878, which originally stood at Cedarburg, Wisconsin, leads to the kind of substantial house a farmer might have built in Wisconsin in the 1890s. The

An overview of Stonefield Village, which consists of 40 historic buildings that typify a Wisconsin farm center in the final decade of the 19th century.

honey house in the backyard stands as a testament to the region's thriving beekeeping industry.

At the heart of the village is a large square bordered by shops that illustrate the range of goods and services available to farm families at the end of the century. There is a general store, which in the 1890s was still the primary source of essential goods, although it faced increasing competition from large mail-order houses like Montgomery Ward and Sears Roebuck. The hardware store, which doubles at Stonefield Village as a harness shop, stocks leather items and the general tools and implements increasingly in demand from both farmers and businessmen in the 1890s. At the drug store, the mainstays are the medicines which the druggist would have prepared by hand with a mortar and pestle form his extensive stock of roots, bark, powders, and oils. However, by the 1890s, rural drug stores were also selling items unrelated to health care.

Like a good rural community of the period, Stonefield Village also boasts a confectionery (ice cream parlor); a jewelry store, featuring furniture and equipment that was used in a store in Horicon, Wisconsin; and a law office, whose equipment includes a chair owned by Wisconsin's Progressive leader, the late Senator Robert M. La Follette. The Bank of Stonefield is modeled after the Fox River Bank of De Pere, Wisconsin, with cages and furniture from a Sauk County bank. The meat market is a reminder of the state's sixth largest industry in the 1890s—meat packing. A millinery shop, where ladies acquired the wide-brimmed hats popular in the period, a two-chair barber shop with wall rack for customers' personal shaving

(*Above*) **The interior of this late-19th-century schoolhouse at Stonefield Village shows how Midwestern educational institutions had progressed from the log cabins of a few decades earlier.**

(**Left**) **Rip-roaring frontier saloons were becoming a distant memory at the end of the 19th century as beer-drinking German immigrants gave many Wisconsin bars—like this one at Stonefield Village—a club-like atmosphere.**

This Stonefield
harness and
hardware store
supplemented its
regular stock with
baby buggies, one of
which is equipped
with an umbrella.

mugs, and other assorted shops complete the picture of a bustling little community with its eye toward the future.

The drug and broom factories, also located on the square, and the nearby cigar plant typify the small local industries that might be found in such communities.

Around the village one finds a variety of other buildings of importance, including the 1896 volunteer firehouse, which is equipped with hand-pumped wagons, a hose cart, and a water wagon; the prefabricated, mail-order jail which was once used at Lone Rock, Wisconsin; a creamery, which relieved the farmer's wife of the drudgery of butter churning; and a telephone exchange, whose magneto system—which still works—handled local and long-distance calls.

Interpretive programs help the visitor experience life in the rural Midwest during the 1890s. Two horse-drawn omnibuses, operating out of the stable, carry visitors over the dirt roads and through the covered bridge. One of the wagons was in service in the 1880s in Luxemburg, Wisconsin; the other was constructed at Stonefield. Old-fashioned candies, ice cream, soda, and sandwiches are sold in period settings. Crafts exhibits and demonstrations are held.

Local initiative in the 1930s prompted the development of the three-sided complex. The section on which Nelson Dewey's home sits was purchased in 1936, whereas the Agricultural Museum, built on the foundations of a Dewey barn, was authorized by the state legislature in 1953 to honor the former governor's early contributions to agriculture. Other governmental donors include the village of Cassville and Grant County. The complex has been operated by the State Historical Society of Wisconsin and the Wisconsin Department of Natural Resources since 1948.

Threshing on a prosperous Wisconsin farm was once a formidable task, but mechanized equipment in the latter portion of the 19th century made the farmer's job much easier.

Old World Wisconsin

During the latter half of the 19th century, the trickle of immigrants that had been coming to the United States became a flood. Wave after wave of Scandinavians settled the tier of North Central states, where the climate and terrain resembled that of their homelands. Germans, too, sought out open territory where they could establish farms. Lesser numbers of Cornish, Irish, Bohemians, Swiss, and other ethnic groups settled near the dwindling and constricted native American population. The resulting ethnic diversity of the Great Lakes states is amply demonstrated at Old World Wisconsin in the Southern Kettle Moraine State Forest near Eagle.

National folkways and preferences in lifestyle, as well as the uniting force of the American ideal, are kept alive by the village's costumed interpreters and special events. The Midsummer Festival in mid-June, for example, continues an ancient Scandinavian tradition at which costumed revelers dance around a Maypole. By contrast, the joyous observance of the Fourth of July includes a greased pole climb and other games, as well as music and oratory that celebrates the quick assimilation of the immigrants into American life.

At Thresheree in September, demonstrators show how threshing was done from the early days of Wisconsin settlement to the era of mechanization. An 1865-style costume ball is held every September. In late October the museum battens down for winter: the last crops are gathered, soap is made, hogs and geese are prepared for market, and an old-fashioned quilting bee is held.

Old World Wisconsin also depicts the state's agricultural heritage from its dawning in the 1840s to the early decades of the 20th century, but it is most revealing of the period around 1880 when farmlife was maturing. Blacksmiths, carpenters, wagonmakers, and other craftsmen demonstrate their skills, while women in spotless aprons and large pleated bonnets discuss with visitors subjects such as clothing, furniture, fine glassware, and the challenge of cooking on a massive wood stove. Through chores like the hand-washing of clothes, the women also illustrate the hard work that farm wives endured—as well as their passion for cleanliness.

The seasonal rhythms are observed. Attendants sow, cultivate, harvest, and store crops and forage. Kitchen gardens provide vegetables for the table. Cows are milked, fowl are fed, and cages and barns are repaired. Pigs root in their pen, and cattle graze in fenced fields. A draft wagon pulled by Morgans, the first domestic breed of horses, moves through the complex.

The mid-summer celebration at Old World Wisconsin includes traditional Scandanavian dances.

More than 50 buildings have been collected from all areas of the state to create a Crossroads Village and Finnish, Danish, Norwegian, and German enclaves, the beginning of an ethnic complex that eventually will be much larger. Currently, eight such traditional "national" farmsteads are preserved in the 576-acre outdoor museum. A walking circuit of 2½ miles includes short nature trails and roads. Trams also carry visitors from one farmstead to another.

The Crossroads Village depicts a typical Wisconsin social and commercial center of the 1870s. The workplaces of artisans such as the blacksmith and wagonmaker may be found here, along with other assorted shops and businesses. Of particular interest are the rooming house—Four Mile House—which was once a stagecoach inn; St. Peter's Church, circa 1839, the First Roman Catholic church in Wisconsin; and the Town Hall. There are several residences in the village, including the Irish Widow's House and the 1858 Greek revival Sanford House.

Three farms are located in the Germanic area. The Pomeranian half-timbered 1856 Schulz House features a large open hearth for cooking and a weaving room. Both the Schultz House and the saltbox-style Turck–Schottler House, circa 1847, are listed on the National Register of Historic Places. The area also boasts a log granary, circa 1865, and a thatched roof barn, circa 1855.

A schoolhouse, built in 1896 and restored to its 1906 appearance, is located in the Norwegian section, but it's the farms that dominate the area. One of the oldest structures at the museum is a pioneer farmhouse of oak logs built by young

Kundt Fossebrekke in 1841. The Kvaale farm, which postdates the Fossebrekke farm by some 20 years, illustrates the refinements that emerged in the region during the 1860s and 1870s; the farmhouse, restored to its 1865 appearance, has a covered porch (*svalgang*) of the type common in Norwegian houses at the time.

The Danish Pederson House, built in 1872 and restored to its 1890 appearance, and the Jensen barn re-create a dairy farm of the period. In the Finnish area, one can find several other examples of turn-of-the-century farms. There is the Jacob Rankinen House, built in 1892, which features chinking between the logs, an unusual construction method. It comes complete with a log outhouse, circa 1910, which is similar to one which stood on the Rankinen farm early in this century. The 1915 Ketola farm depicts an established dairy farm about 1915. It features a sauna—a standard component of any good Finnish farm. After working up a good sweat in the sauna, a Finn would typically roll in the snow or bathe in an icy stream.

A public–private partnership created Old World Wisconsin in 1976 as a state project for the national bicentennial, but the idea dates back to 1956 when German-born Hans Kuether proposed a village of half-timbered Pomeranian houses. This idea was expanded to include the multinational, multicultural concept of Old World Wisconsin proposed by Richard W. E. Perrin, who in 1964 was instrumental in getting the participation of the State Historical Soceity of Wisconsin and initiating the search for a site.

(*Left*) **This modest 1885 house from Hubbleton, Wisconsin, is named for an Irish widow, Mary Hafford, who lived there. The house was designed to fit a narrow lot with room for expansion if space permitted.**

(*Opposite*) **Doug Hennig plays the part of a prosperous mid-19th-century farmer at the Koepsell Farm at Old World Wisconsin.**

Living History Farms

By the 1870s, frontier Iowa had given way to towns and villages. The rugged life portrayed in the Ioway Indian Village and the 1850s settlement at the Living History Farms in Des Moines (see *Part II: The Developing Nation, The Northeast*) stand in dramatic contrast to the more refined lifestyle at the museum's 1875 Walnut Hill, a re-created rural village. Here, a lawyer with a library full of lawbooks is available to serve his neighbors' needs, as is a doctor with surgical implements. There is a bank and a newspaper/printing shop that turns out a weekly local newspaper. There is a general store where folks congregate to swap stories and talk about the weather. It is jam-packed with everything from stick candy to harnesses and also doubles as the post office. There is a schoolhouse, which is equipped with stove heat in the winter, maps and slates where the pupils can work their problems, and a flagpole out front. There is even a mansion built by a railroad magnate, Martin Flynn, in 1870. It includes a library, two parlors, a dining room, and bedrooms. A Prairie Gothic interdenominational church (visited by Pope John Paul II in 1979) provides for the spiritual needs of the community.

The museum also illustrates the changes in farming during the latter half of the 19th century. The house at the 1900-style farm blends traditional fixtures, such as a wood-burning stove and a trundle bed, with innovative equipment, such as a hand-powered washing machine and a water pump. Of course, canning, cooking, washing, and other chores still required long hours of hot toil, but a pump organ in the parlor provided a pleasant respite for the family when the day's toil was done.

Around the farm one can find the innovations that came along by 1900 to maximize the farmer's productivity. A steam engine is in use to thresh grain and perform other chores, and a pulley has been installed in the barn to raise hay from a horse-drawn wagon to the loft, where it is stored. Gardening, hoeing, hand harvesting, butchering livestock, and mending fences kept the turn-of-the-century farmer busy from dawn to dusk. His wife was no less busy with outdoors tasks, as well as with household work.

Subsequent 20th-century innovations are depicted at the museum's Farm of Today and Tomorrow. They include the earth-sheltered William G. Murray solar home and the Henry A. Wallace Crop Center, where modern techniques and hybrids can be examined.

(*Opposite*) **A pump well was a valuable asset to housewives on turn-of-the century Iowa farms.**

Important documents are carefully transcribed by hand in this lawyer's office at Walnut Hill, a re-created rural village, circa 1875, at Living History Farms.

(*Left*) **The post office at Walnut Hill is located in the general store, which is stocked with 19th-century merchandise.**

(*Below*) **On Iowa farms around the turn of the century, the kitchen was an all-purpose workroom. Its warm stove also made it a popular family room in winter.**

Ford Museum and Greenfield Village

Over the course of the 19th century—and into the 20th—rapid advances in technology brought America's passion for gadgets to a peak. Laundering moved from the drudgery of the scrub board to hand-cranked washing machines to rotary machines run by electric power. Electricity revolutionized American life. So did the advent of rapid means of transportation—the locomotive, automobile, and airplane—and communications—the telegraph, telephone, radio, and later television.

No place demonstrates the impact of the technological revolution better than the Henry Ford Museum and Greenfield Village, in Dearborn, Michigan. The complex, which covers 254 acres, is divided into two distinct sections: the museum, a building whose entrance is modeled after Philadelphia's Independence Hall; and the village, an open-air museum where a variety of past eras come to life through historic buildings and costumed interpreters.

Both museum and village focus on the technology that ingenious Americans like Thomas A. Edison and Orville and Wilbur Wright have produced, and the impact they have had on society. While early American artifacts are included, the museum concentrates primarily on the period when the nation was maturing.

One of the complex's major areas of interest is transportation—cars, trains, and planes—not surprising, considering that the museum's founder was Henry Ford. In 1987, the first major renovation in 50 years allocated nearly half of the museum building to "The Automobile in American Life." This exhibition shows the enormous impact that cars have had on the way Americans have lived, worked, and played. The museum's collection of classic and antique automobiles—one of the most extensive in the world—is on display along with full-size buildings of interest to automobile aficionados, like a 1946 highway diner, a 1940s Texaco gasoline station, a 1950s drive-in theater, and a 1960s Holiday Inn guest room. Large graphic elements, film clips, and an extensive collection of car models add to the ambience.

The formative years of the airplane industry are also explored at the museum through displays that include the trimotor Ford plane covered with corrugated metal that flew Adm. Richard E. Byrd over the South Pole in November 1929 and a plane in which Gen. Jimmy Doolittle raced as a junior officer in the years prior to World War II.

(Opposite) **A pair of cyclists visit the shop where Wilbur and Orville Wright turned out bicycles and built the first successful powered airplane.**

(Below) **This is a reconstruction of the building, often called the Mack Avenue plant, where Henry Ford produced his first cars.**

The "Automobile in American Life" exhibit, which occupies almost half of the Henry Ford Museum, examines the influence of motor transport on all aspects of American society.

Bicycles, linked to the history of the development of flight by the Wright brothers—whose bicycle shop is located in Greenfield Village—were an intermediate stage of transportation in American life, now reduced mainly to a sporting and exercise role. Among the historic bikes in the Henry Ford Museum is a 10-man example of "far-out" design.

Railroads were instrumental in binding the nation together from coast to coast; at the museum, examples of locomotives progress from the time when passengers took pot shots at buffalo while riding westward across the Plains. Among the museum's treasures is a 600-ton coal-burning locomotive, one of the largest ever built. A train dating from 1873 loads passengers at a 19th-century station just inside Greenfield Village and chugs on a circular track on the perimeter of the complex.

While the Henry Ford Museum and Greenfield Village complex is rich in its transportation displays, its wide-ranging collections cover a host of other topics, such as lighting and communications, power and machinery, agriculture, decorative arts, home arts, and musical instruments. Among its wealth of artifacts are a cast iron Gothic engine, circa 1857, which helped introduce the industrial revolution; a Massey-Harris Model 20 combine, which revolutionized the harvesting of grain; a "streamlined" 1930s kitchen; furniture (including the rocking chair in which President Abraham Lincoln was sitting at Ford's Theatre when he was assassinated on April 14, 1865); office machines; and radio and television sets.

Visitors may participate in a number of exhibits. They can mount a high-wheel bicycle, for example, tap out a message on the telegraph, or sit on the stools of a 1930s diner.

Meanwhile, life moves at a leisurely pace at Greenfield Village. A man in suspenders and cap pushes a cart laden with jars of candy past the brick Wright Cycle Shop (known as the "birthplace of aviation" because Orville and Wilbur there conceived of the first motorized manned airplane). A Model T Ford chugs past the white-columned Town Hall. Children play 19th-century games on the Village Green in front of the Martha–Mary Chapel. Merino sheep graze at Firestone Farm. The shop girls at Cohen Millinery use feathers, ribbons, and flowers to make the large, effusively ornamented women's hats that were popular around 1900. Meanwhile, the differences between carding and machine treatments of wool are explored at the Plymouth Carding Mill. Many other aspects of turn-of-the-century life invite visitor attention: bike safety, the production of tinware and glass, livestock breeding, and the operation of looms, to name but a few.

A rich assortment of historic structures provides the setting for this exploration, with the birthplace of Henry Ford taking pride of place. It is a typical Midwestern farmhouse, with small rooms and simple furnishings. In the 1870s, Ford was a student in the one-room Scotch Settlement School which faces the Village Green.

The memory of Thomas A. Edison, Ford's friend and neighbor, is strong at the Menlo Park Compound, in whose workshops Edison produced inventions such as the electric light and phonograph; the Sarah Jordan boardinghouse, where he once lived; and his Fort Myers laboratory. Down another street,

Costumed interpreters give life to Greenfield Village, a collection of more than 90 historic structures from various parts of the nation.

past a large statue of Edison, stands the 1888 Edison Illuminating Co. from Detroit, one of the first electrical power plants in the world. The huge machinery that brought electricity into households is visible through the windows.

In its tribute to America's technological progress, the village also looks back to the pioneering spirit of the preindustrial period. Tobacco—the nation's first profitable export—and the culture it fostered are examined at the Susquehanna Plantation, while demonstrations of canning, food preparation, and housekeeping enliven the 1760s Connecticut saltbox house. The classical revival Noah Webster House stands as a testament to the noted educator and lexicographer who in the early

19th century completed what became the standard American dictionary. There is also the Courthouse of Logan County, Illinois, where Abe Lincoln practiced as a lawyer; the 1850s Eagle Tavern, where visitors can dine on period china and pistol-grip silverware; and the one-room log cabin birthplace of William Holmes McGuffey, whose textbook taught generation after generation of 19th-century children to read.

While it is fascinating to see these mementos of American history, it is the nation's zest for change that most visitors take with them from the Henry Ford Museum and Greenfield Village. An enthusiasm for the new and a quest for the better, an urge to explore and a desire to experiment have characterized the American people from the earliest days of colonization. No doubt that spirit of innovation will continue to propel America's progress as the nation moves into the 1990s and on into the 21st century.

ADDITIONAL INFORMATION

THE NORTHEAST

1 Belcourt Castle,
pp. 168–171
Newport, RI 02840-4288
(401) 846-0669

2 Genesee Country Museum,
pp. 52–55
P.O. Box 310
Mumford, NY 14511
(716) 538-6822

**3 Gettysburg National
Military Park,** p. 91
Gettysburg, PA 17325
(717) 334-1124

4 Fort Ticonderoga,
pp. 34–36
Box 390
Ticonderoga, N.Y. 20883
(518) 585-2821

5 Hancock Shaker Village,
pp. 56–59
P.O. Box 898
Pittsfield, MA 01202
(413) 443-0188

**6 Independence National
Historic Park,** pp. 30–32
313 Walnut Street
Philadelphia, PA 19106
(215) 597-7120

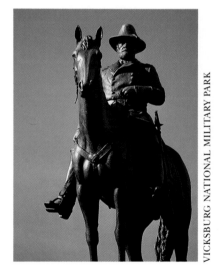

VICKSBURG NATIONAL MILITARY PARK

7 Mystic Seaport Museum,
pp. 160–163
P.O. Box 6000
Mystic, CT 06355
(203) 572-0711

**1 The Preservation Society of
Newport County,** pp. 168–171
118 Mill Street
Newport, RI 02840
(401) 847-1000

8 Old Sturbridge Village,
pp. 44–48
1 Old Sturbridge Village Road
Sturbridge, MA 01566
(508) 347-3362

9 Plimoth Plantation,
pp. 19–22
P.O. Box 1620
Plymouth, MA 02360
(508) 746-1622

**10 Saratoga National Historic
Park,** p. 36
RD 2, Box 33
Stillwater, NY 12170
(518) 664-9821

11 Shelburne Museum,
pp. 49–51, 164–167
Route 7
Shelburne, VT 05482
(802) 985-3346

**12 Valley Forge National
Historic Park,** p. 37
P.O. Box 953
Valley Forge, PA 19481-0953
(215) 783-1000

THE SOUTHEAST

**13 Appomattox Court House
National Historic Park,**
pp. 94–95
P.O. Box 218
Appomattox, VA 24522
(804) 352-8987

14 Colonial Williamsburg,
pp. 23–25
P.O. Box B
Williamsburg, VA 23187
(800) H-I-S-T-O-R-Y

**15 Florewood River
Plantation,** pp. 75–77
P.O. Box 680
Fort Loring Road
Greenwood, MS 38930
(601) 455-3821

16 Historic Charleston,
pp. 79–82
Chamber of Commerce
P.O. Box 975
Charleston, SC 29403
(803) 577-2510

17 Historic Savannah,
pp. 83–86
Savannah Visitors Center
301 North Broad Street
Savannah, GA 31499
(912) 944-0456

LINCOLN'S NEW SALEM HISTORIC SITE

**18 Jamestown Settlement
(Jamestown Festival Park),**
pp. 16–18
P.O. Drawer JF
Williamsburg, VA 23187
(804) 229-1607

**18 & 24 Jamestown National
Historic Site/Yorktown
Battlefield,** pp. 16–18, 38, 39
Colonial National Historic
Park
P.O. Box 210
Yorktown, VA 23690
(804) 898-3400

**19 Manassas National
Battlefield Park,** p. 88
6511 Sudley Road
Manassas, VA 22110
(703) 754-7109

**20 New Market Battlefield
Park,** pp. 92–93
P.O. Box 1864
New Market, VA 22844
(703) 740-3101

21 Historic St. Augustine,
pp. 12–15
St. Augustine Chamber of
Commerce
P.O. Drawer O
St Augustine, FL 32085
(904) 829-5681

**22 Vicksburg National
Military Park,** p. 89
3201 Clay Street
Vicksburg, MS 39180
(601) 636-0583

23 Westville, pp. 72–74
P.O. Box 1850
Lumpkin, GA 31815
(912) 838-6310

24 Yorktown Victory Center,
pp. 38–39
Route 238
Yorktown, VA 23690
(804)-887-1776

THE MIDWEST

25 Cherokee Heritage Center,
pp. 103–106
P.O. Box 515
Tahlequah, OK 74465
(918) 456-6007

**26 Henry Ford Museum &
Greenfield Village,**
pp. 186–189
P.O. Box 1970
Dearborn, MI 48121
(313) 271-1620

**27 Fort Davis National
Historic Site,** pp. 145–147
Box 1456
Fort Davis, TX 79734
(915) 426-3224

**28 Fort Union Trading Post
National Historic Site,**
pp. 112–114
Buford Route, Williston, ND
58801
(701) 572-9083

**29 Deadwood Historic
District,** pp. 134–136
c/o Deadwood-Lead Area
Chamber of Commerce
735 Main Street
Deadwood, SD 57332
(605) 578-1876

VALLEY FORGE NATIONAL HISTORIC PARK

30 Lincoln's New Salem Historic Site, pp. 64–67
RR1, Box 244A
Petersburg, IL 62675

31 Living History Farms, pp. 61–63, 182–185
2600 NW 111th Street
Urbandale, IO 50322
(515) 278-5286

32 Old Cowtown Museum, pp. 127–129
1871 Sim Park Drive
Wichita, KS 67203
(316) 264-0671

33 Old World Wisconsin, pp. 179–181
South 103 West Highway 67
Eagle, WI 53119
(414) 594-2116

34 Ranching Heritage Center, pp. 149–151
P.O. Box 4040
Lubbock, TX 79409
(806) 742-2498

35 Stonefield Village, pp. 175–178
Box 147
Cassville, WI 53806
(608) 725-5210

36 Stuhr Museum of the Prarie Pioneer, pp. 137–141
3133 West Highway 34
Grand Island, NE 68801
(308) 381-5316

THE WEST

37 Bent's Old Fort Historic Site, pp. 118–122
35110 Highway 194 East
La Junta, CO 81050-9523
(719) 384-2596

38 Fort Clatsop National Memorial, pp. 108–111
Route 3, Box 604-FC
Astoria, OR 97103
(503) 861-2471

39 Fort Laramie National Historic Site, pp.141–144
P.O. Box 86
Ft. Laramie, WY 8212
(307) 837-2221

40 Fort Nisqually, pp.115–117
Point Defiance
Tacoma, WA 98407
(206) 591-5339

41 Grant–Kohrs Ranch National Historic Center, pp. 152–155
P.O. Box 790
Deer Lodge, MT 59722
(406) 846-3388
(406) 846-2070 (Visitors Center)

OLD COWTOWN MUSEUM

42 Tombstone, pp. 130–133
P.O. Box 216
Tombstone, AZ 85638
(602) 457-3311

43 Sutter's Fort, pp. 123–126
111 I Street
Sacramento, CA 95814
(916) 445-4209

44 Taos Pueblo, pp. 100–102
Tourism Department
P.O. Box 1846
Taos, NM 87571
(505) 758-8626

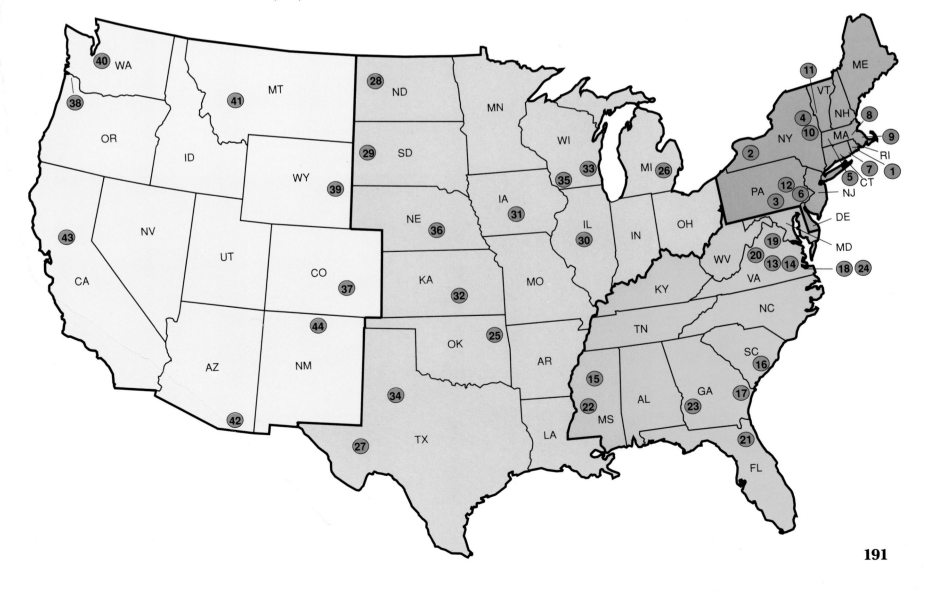

ACKNOWLEDGEMENTS

Grateful appreciation is made to the following individuals for their assistance in the creation of this book:

Adirondack Museum, Ann Carroll; Alabama Historical Commission, Jack Stell; Alaskaland, Penny Morton; Appomattox Court House National Historical Site, Mr. Wilson; Arizona State Park, Hollis Cook; Belcourt Castle, Mrs. Ruth Tinney; Bent's Old Fort Historic Site, Don Hill; Boot Hill Museum, Jim Sherer & Brownie Harris; Chesepeake and Ohio Canal National Historic Park, Rita Knox; Chelan County Historical Museum, Jim Wilson; The Cherokee National Historical Society, Inc., Debbie Duvall; The Colonial Williamsburg Foundation, Catherine Grosfils; Eckley Miner's Village Museum, Elaine Rauffman; Edison National Historic Site, Terry Jung; Fort Laramie National Historic Site, John Burns; Fort Nisqually, Steve Anderson; Fort Seldon, Jose Guzman; Fort Ticonderoga, James Nicholas; Fort Union Trading Post, Paul Hedren; Genesee Country Museum, Jo Betz; Gettysburg National Military Park; Grant-Kohrs Ranch, Cheryl Clemmenson; Hancock Shaker Village, Beatrice Snyder; Henry Ford Museum and Greenfield Village, Laurie Dick; Historic New Harmony, Julienne Rutherford; Historic Speedwell, Sarah Haskins; Historic St. Augustine Preservation, Rita O'Brien; Historic Wichita-Sedgwick County Inc.; Jamestown-Yorktown Foundation, Debby Padgett; Landis Valley Museum, Daniel B. Reibel; Lincoln's New Salem State Historic Site, David Hedrick; The Living History Association, James Dassatti; Living History Farms, Miriam Dunlap; Mississippi Department of Natural Resources, Diane Manton; Mount Washington Cog Railway, Robert Clemens; Mystic Seaport Museum, Lisa Brownwell; New York State Department of Economic Development, John C. Cusano; New York State Historical Association, Farmers Museum, David R. Porter; Old Abolene Town, Eleanor Green; Old Cowtown Museum, Elizabeth Kennedy; Ohio Historical Society, Mariann Bayus; Old North Hill Street Historic District, Carol King; Old Sturbridge Village, Rick Orluk, Carole Gigg; Old Town San Diego Historical Park, Mark Forgensen; Pella Historical Village, Patsy Sadler; Pennsylvania Bureau of Travel Marketing, LynnSherron; Philadelphia Convention and Visitors Bureau, Susan Oates; Plymouth County Development Council, Janet Ramsay; The Portsmouth Press, Russ Kendall; Prarie Historical Society, Inc., Lola Robson; Prarie Village, Myron Downs; Ranching Heritage Association, Tommy Morman; Saratoga National Historical Park, Eileen Gannon; Savannah Chamber of Commerce, Terry Stacey; Shelburne Museum, Shelburne Vermont, Audrey Ritter; South Carolina Historical Society, Steve Hoffius; Spring Mill State Park, Tim Cordell; State Historical Association; State Historical Society of Wisconsin, Robert Granflaten, John Reilley, Tammy L. Tritz; Stonefield Village State Historical Society, Mary Granflaten; Stuhr Museum of the Prarie Pioneer, Lew Cole; St. Augustine Chamber of Commerce, Cora Lee Pomar; St. Augustine Historic District, Jean Rosenthal, Susan Engelmann, Photography; St. Augustine Preservation Board, Cookie O'Brien; Taos Pueblo Tourism Department; Tennessee Tourist Development; Valley Forge Country Convention and Visitors Bureau, Barbara Lenman; Virginia Division of Tourism, Pamela Jewell; West Point Museum, David Meschutt; Westville Historic Handicrafts, Inc., Patty Cannington; Yosemite National Park.

PHOTO CREDITS

u.l.= upper left; u.r. = upper right; u.m. = upper middle; l.l. = lower left; l.r. = lower right; l.m. = lower middle; m = middle

Belcourt Castle 159 (u.l.), 168
Alan Briere, 32 (l.l.), 60 (l.l.), 64-70 , 75-88, 90-95,156-157, 159, (l.r.),160-163, 175, 176 (top), 190 (l.m., u.r.)
The Cherokee National Historical Society 99, 103, 104-105, 106
Colonial National Historic Park, 38, 39
The Colonial Williamsburg Foundation, 25
Suzanne Engelman, 11 (l.l., l.r.), 12, 14, 15, 29 (l.l., l.r.), 31, 32 (l.r.)
Fort Clatsop National Memorial 108
Genesee Country Museum/Ruby Foote 43 (l.r.), 52, 53, 54, 55
Hancock Shaker Village 4-5, 42, 57, 58, 59
Brownie Harris, 8-10, 19-22
The Henry Ford Museum and Greenfield Village 174 (u.l.), 186-189, 192
Historic Wichita-Sedgwick County, Inc. "Old Cowtown Museum"/Ricardo Reitmeyer 122(u.r.), 127-129, 191
Jamestown Settlement (Jamestown Festival Park), 11 (u.m.), 16, 17, 18
Living History Farms 2-3, 6, 60 (u.r.), 61-63, 174 (m), 182-185
The National Park Service, 28, 29 (u.m.), 30, 33 (l.r.), 36
New York State Department of Economic Development, 33 (l.l.), 34, 35
Old Sturbridge Village/Robert S. Arnold, 40, 43 (l.l.), 44-48
Preservation Society of Newport 169-173
Radeka 96-97,107 ,109-112,114-119,121,122 (l.l., l.r.), 123-126, 130-148, 152-155
Ranching Heritage Association 149-151
Shelburne Museum, 43 (top), 49, 164,166,167
SuperStock International, Inc., 13, 23, 24, 26, 27, 51, 56, 158, 165
Taos Pueblo 100-102
Valley Forge Area Convention and Visitors Bureau, 33 (u.r.), 37, 190 (u.l.)
Vicksburg Convention and Visitors Bureau, 89
Wisconsin State Historical Society 174 (r.), 176 (bottom), 178-181
Westville Historic Handicrafts, Inc., 71, 73, 74

THE HENRY FORD MUSEUM & GREENFIELD VILLAGE